I0063064

EXIT BY FORCE

The Five-Step Method to Maximize Founder
Value and Become the Most Attractive
Business to Acquire

ANAND NARAYAN

EXIT BY FORCE

The Five-Step Method to Maximize Founder
Value and Become the Most Attractive
Business to Acquire

First published in 2024 by Intellectual Perspective Press
© Copyright Anand Narayan

All rights reserved. No part of this publication may be reproduced, stored in or introduced into a retrieval system, or transmitted, in any form, or by any means (electronic, mechanical, photocopying, recording or otherwise) without the prior written permission of the Publisher.

The right of Anand Narayan to be identified as the author of this work has been asserted in accordance with the Copyright, Designs and Patents Act 1988.

This book is sold subject to the condition that it shall not, by way of trade or otherwise, be lent, resold, hired out, or otherwise circulated without the publisher's prior consent in any form of binding or cover other than that in which it is published and without a similar condition including this condition being imposed on the subsequent Purchaser.

The purpose of this book is to educate and entertain. The author and Intellectual Perspective Press shall have neither liability nor responsibility to any person or entity with respect to any loss or damage caused, or alleged to have been caused, directly or indirectly, by the information contained in this book.

To find out more about our authors and books visit:
www.intellectualperspective.com

Book Interior and E-book Design by Amit Dey
(amitdey2528@gmail.com)

CONTENTS

INTRODUCTION XI
LEARNER TO MASTER

EPISODE 1 2
THE PATH YOU CHOOSE IS YOURS ALONE

EPISODE 2 31
TRUST IN THE FORCE

EPISODE 3 143
YOUR FOCUS DETERMINES YOUR REALITY

PRAISE FOR EXIT BY FORCE

Participating in the Exit By FORCE Accelerator was a transformative experience. It enabled us to streamline our operations significantly, enhancing efficiency and scalability. The strategic insights and tools provided by the accelerator were instrumental in refining our business model and optimizing our resource allocation. As a result, we successfully exited at an impressive 15X multiple—a testament to the robust growth and value enhancement driven by our partnership with Kenobi Capital. This program is a game-changer for any tech company aiming to maximize its market potential and achieve an optimal exit strategy.

— Nani Ramanujam, Serial Entrepreneur with multiple exits, including IT Trailblazers and ITTDigital

Successful businesses excel at understanding their clients' needs and creating products to solve those problems. What many business owners fail to grasp is that the business they are building can also be a solution to an investor's or corporate buyer's problem. Anand Narayan helps business owners think of their business as a product that not only solves the buyer's problem but also makes it easy to acquire. These are crucial insights all business owners should understand.

— Callum Laing, Entrepreneur, Investor, and Best-Selling Author

You don't make money running businesses; you make money when you sell them. The right time to sell is now, and all the reasons you think of not to sell are probably the things buyers want to hear. I support anything that can help entrepreneurs understand how to exit successfully and democratize wealth into the hands of entrepreneurs who are the change agents in our society. This book does just that; congratulations to Anand on the new book.

— Jeremy Harbour, Founder and CEO of Unity Group &
Associated Companies

I wholeheartedly endorse Anand Narayan's Exit By FORCE framework as a transformative tool for entrepreneurs seeking impactful exits. As someone who has successfully led Kaia Health and had a personal exit and now at the helms of Ciba Health, one of the fastest-growing digital health companies, I can personally attest to the immense value of strategic guidance in scaling and optimizing a business for acquisition. Anand's expertise is a game-changer for any entrepreneur committed to unlocking their business's full potential and maximizing its value.

— Innocent Clement, MD, MPH, MBA,
Founder and CEO of Ciba Health

With over 35 years of experience in leading multinational and publicly listed companies, I've learned that success lies in strategic foresight and operational excellence. While advising companies looking for acquisitions, these were the exact checks I emphasized. Anand Narayan's Exit By FORCE framework is a vital resource for business leaders aiming to enhance their company's value and execute a seamless exit. His methodology provides the clarity and direction needed to transform operational strengths into a compelling narrative for buyers, ensuring that you don't just exit, but you exit on your terms.

— Dinakar Adhyam,
Managing Director of Saint Gobain Ltd

As an innovator and venture capitalist, I've seen firsthand the importance of strategic planning in scaling and exiting companies. Anand Narayan's Exit By FORCE framework is a crucial resource for any entrepreneur or business leader aiming to navigate the complexities of an exit. His insights into aligning clinical, operational, and financial expertise with strategic goals are invaluable, particularly in the healthcare sector. This book is an essential guide for achieving a successful and impactful exit.

— Manish Bhandari, MD, Managing Partner/Founder
at Angel Physicians Fund and Chief of Innovation
at St. Elizabeth Healthcare

I dedicate this book to small business owners like my father, who risk it all in search of a better future.

I hope that the ideas in this book reward you for the blood, sweat, and years you've put into creating value for everyone around you.

Also, I thank my sister, who encouraged and helped me write this book.

INTRODUCTION: LEARNER TO MASTER

"I was but the learner, now I am the master."

– Darth Vader

On a warm sunny day, I was soaring high in a Cessna Skyhawk 172 heading back to Austin International Airport with my instructor beside me. I had just learned how to land a plane—a super stressful experience—and was heading back after a call from my wife. She was about to go into labor. Later, I found out it was a false alarm, but at that moment, it felt very real, and I was rushing to get home. My instructor was a 23-year-old who had recently completed private pilot training and certified flight instructor training. I was literally the second student. I was training with a reputable school in Austin, and didn't think much of it. While inbound to landing, we received a strange command. We were to land on the left runway, but were told to follow the plane heading for the right runway.

My flight instructor was taking over at the time; there was just too much traffic. As we were turning in, following the plane, we passed the left runway flight path, and continued following the large airliner going to the right runway. I knew something didn't add up—shouldn't we have turned toward the left runway by now? But I let it go. The instructor must know what she's doing, correct? That was my first mistake. I should have been vocal. We continued without clearance for the right runway, and the air traffic controller came blaring over the frequency that we were getting into a dangerous situation. We were supposed to cut in left, but were instead crossing the right runway flight path with another plane inbound. The instructor got stressed out, made a U-turn while crossing the right flight path, and ended up back into the right runway flight path, this time heading for our runway. Again, I didn't say anything, doesn't that seem obvious not to fly through the right runway flight path, I mean, we could see the inboard plane heading toward us. That really threw off the airport, they asked all inbound planes to take evasive actions, as we followed step-by-step headings until we landed.

That's when I resolved: when the stakes are high, always be in control.

This applies to my life, my family, my wealth, and my business. While we landed safely, I will never forget how scary that day was. I trusted my life to a 23-year-old "expert" who was as green as it gets. I will never be in a situation again where I allow "experts" to control my life, especially when the stakes are so high.

In business, while the stakes are not life-threatening, they are too high to allow your destiny to be controlled by others. I made this mistake when I was young and sold my first company. I let life control my destiny. The offer came when my father and I were not prepared to sell. We didn't educate ourselves, and let the buyers and our advisors control the process. We sold our company for 15X EBITDA (Earnings Before Interest, Taxes, Depreciation, and Amortization), a valuation that seemed too good to be true, and almost lost it all. We let life "happen" to us when the stakes were so high—the lifeblood of our family and our wealth was transferring hands, and we had no control. Throughout this book, you will find the mistakes we made in our first sale and the grueling fight that is ongoing, three years later, to get our money. You will learn from a real-life scenario that almost destroyed our generational wealth.

I am a trained chemical engineer from Rutgers University and served as a nuclear propulsion officer in the US Navy. I joined IT Trailblazers, the company that we almost lost, in 2016 when it was earning $12 million in revenue. Over the next four years, I was appointed the chief operating officer, the right hand to my father, the founder of the company. By 2020, when we exited, we were earning $65 million in revenue, and I had completed my MBA at Cornell University. We went from a small business to a medium-sized company that was professionally run. While the FORCE methodology was not yet named, it was the framework I used to scale the business.

In 2020, after the sale of IT Trailblazers, I co-founded ITTDigital with my father. We grew the business to $10 million and exited in 2023, this time with a more reasonable EBITDA multiple valuation, and this time in control of the situation. As we positioned ourselves, I read every M&A book I could get my hands on: all the get-rich-quick books, the buy-a-business-for-$1 books, the private equity books telling you how to screw over small businesses, and the advisor books selling bullshit services without ever running a business. I read all the books written from a seller's perspective that told me how to build wealth at sale and showcase the value of my business. While some were helpful, they seemed written by non-business owners—I just couldn't relate. After making my own mistakes running the exit process of the first business, my father blindly trusting that I knew what I was doing, I excelled the second time. We Maximized Founder Value under the most favorable terms with the sale of ITTDigital. We sold for a 10X multiple of EBITDA, and controlled every aspect of the exit process.

I decided to write this book for the small business owner who is looking to move on to their next adventure. It could be to retire, to start a new business, or to take some cards off the table. We sold our first business because we got a great offer, one that was too good to be true. We were not planning to sell or adequately prepared, and look what happened. The second time around, we positioned ourselves for a sale, not looking for it, but we were at the right place, at the right time, and we were ready!

This book is for YOU, the risk-takers of the world, those who don't follow the typical conventions of society: go to a good school, get a job, buy your forever home, pay fees for wealth management— blah, blah, blah. The book is organized into three Episodes. I'm a die-hard *Star Wars* fan and will try to keep the references to a minimum. I got lucky that my framework fits into FORCE. It didn't happen by design. The first Episode will walk you through five myths that most business owners believe in; the second will dive deep into the FORCE methodology; and the third Episode will show you how to execute on it.

Again, this book is written with YOU in mind, the small business owner, whether you are earning $3 million in revenue or $20 million. This book is about how to control the exit process, maximize your generational wealth, avoid common pitfalls, and do it all with peace of mind that you are doing the best thing for your family. You have put blood, sweat, and years into your business and should be rewarded for it.

The market out there is a nightmare. It's not an easy journey. Most of the folks in the acquisition arena are trying to screw you, like they screwed us and thousands of others. The rest are trying to sell you a bullshit service when they have never even incorporated a company. Really? You're going to teach me how to sell my business, useless MBA graduate with a fancy title?

Full disclosure: I want YOU to be successful. You want you to be successful. We have aligned interests. I've been in your shoes. I'm writing this book to support small business owners around the world. Whether you are in construction, lawn mowing, caring for senior citizens, running a daycare, or a small tech business (like ITTDigital), this book will guide you along the journey to get the most out of your business. I've been deceived. I've fought a three-year lawsuit. I've seen what that does to the founders, extended family (being the son myself), employees, clients, and stakeholders. I never want to see that happen to anyone's business or family ever again.

I hope this book serves you well and lines your pockets with millions of dollars or republic credits, if that's worth anything in your galaxy. But if nothing else, I hope it protects you from all the bad actors that are waiting to pounce and take advantage of you. Trust me, it could happen to you, just like it happened to me and countless others. I know this book might insult a lot of professionals, but hey, it's a reality check for them. You've built a wonderful business; I've built a wonderful business. Now let's make it worth our while!

Read this book, take action, and join me along my terrible first exit and super successful second exit. Learn from the several businesses I've helped along the way.

I hope you reach out to me. Get connected when you start your exit journey. Use me as a resource—I'm always happy to help small business owners. If nothing else, please share your story. Tell me how you defied the world of traditional selling, kept money in your pockets, controlled the entire process, and Exited By FORCE.

This book is my attempt to pass down all of my learnings, mine and other small business owners', so that you can get the same results. Throughout this book I am going to include a few freebies, also known as Weapons, so you have everything you need in your arsenal. **Check them out at ExitByFORCE.com/Weapons**. It's lonely at the top, it's even lonelier when you are attempting something as crazy as a business exit. This book will guide you on your way to glory.

On a side note, I had a baby girl a week after that flight incident, and as of writing this book, live in a penthouse in Austin, TX, a happy family of three.

May the FORCE be with you!

①

THE PATH YOU CHOOSE IS YOURS ALONE

Embarking on the journey to exit your business is deeply personal and unique. Every decision you make, every challenge you overcome, and every milestone you reach is part of a path only you can navigate.

This episode will guide you through understanding your readiness, the importance of planning ahead, and how to position yourself for success. Remember, the choices you make today will shape your future and legacy.

The path you choose is yours alone, so let's make it count.

MYTH 1: SUCCESS TODAY MEANS AN EFFORTLESS EXIT TOMORROW

You've built a thriving business from the ground up. It was more than just a venture; it was a testament to your vision and perseverance. Night after night, you traded sleep for strategy, and stability for the exhilarating uncertainty of entrepreneurship. Now, as you stand at the precipice of a successful enterprise, a new question emerges from the shadows of your achievement: what next?

For many founders like you, the answer extends beyond expansion or new ventures. It's about legacy, about translating business success into personal and financial freedom. Not to worry—we will revisit the topic of freedom toward the end of the book.

Many entrepreneurs don't think about exit strategies seriously. However, it's crucial to recognize the importance of having an exit strategy, whether you plan to exit soon or not. Maybe it's time to consider an exit—not out of necessity but because it might be the optimal conclusion to this chapter of your life. Or, perhaps, your kids have vehemently refused to take over the business, leaving you with no other option.

Navigating the transition from owner to seller introduces a complex set of challenges; challenges you haven't faced before. Despite the success of the venture, the path to selling your business is fraught with valuation equations, buyers' negotiations, and the emotional weight of letting go of your creation.

In this era, marked by one of the greatest wealth transfers in history, your business is one among many in the marketplace. And while it's not easy on the ears, here's some truth juice for you: only a select few businesses, one out of every ten, sell on terms that founders feel are truly rewarding. Many end up feeling short-changed, burdened by broker fees, and tangled in less-than-ideal agreements.[1,2,3] Remember that exit undergoing a lawsuit that I mentioned in the introduction, less than ideal is an understatement, so far it's costed us half a million dollars and counting. All to a legal firm, sitting in their fancy offices, laughing at us; all because we were not prepared for how much the legalese mattered.

How, then, do you make your business a unicorn in the crowded marketplace? How do you ensure that it not only attracts attention but commands a premium? There's a predictable journey that you will go through to pursue a wonderful exit experience with success, a sense of accomplishment, and no regrets. We will explore the four types of small business exits in **Episode 3**.

This book is your navigator. I'm on your side, I'm a guide that wants you to be successful. However, The Path You Choose Is Yours Alone. The decisions you make today affect your family and your future generations, not mine; I've already done that. As you continue reading, I'll equip you with the necessary tools and strategies to position your business as a prime target for acquisition, enhancing its inherent value and appeal to prospective buyers. You'll learn how to transfer your years of hard work into a lucrative exit strategy and get your well-earned reward.

However, the path was not without its obstacles. I've faced, as you will, tough negotiations, constant timeline delays, and major setbacks, with each party having a different version of success.

Here's what you really need to know. It's the strategic, well-considered actions that significantly amplify your ability to exit on your terms. Don't sit back and relax, and assume that a buyer will find you; if that happens, it's too good to be true, and you're letting life happen to you, just the way that I did. Even if everything is going great, and you're sleeping on your dollar bills, life can change very quickly. In a matter of weeks, I lost control of a $65 million empire. Success today does not mean success tomorrow; you need to plan for it, put effort into it, and success will follow.

As you continue reading, you will uncover the "Exit By FORCE" strategy, a framework designed to empower you to steer your exit process confidently and profitably. It will take effort, and it's a journey you have to walk, but you're not alone! My mom and I summited Mount Kilimanjaro on her fifty-seventh birthday, and as the guide said, *Pole Pole* (Pol-ay, Pol-ay), which means slowly, slowly, one foot over the other. The only way is up. Come join me over here.

FORCE Exercise: Reflect on your goals and the future you envision for yourself.

- Where do you see yourself in the future?
- What would you love to do now if you didn't have to run your business?
- How does this future align with your business and exit timeline?

Notes:

MYTH 2: EFFORT = VALUE

You've nurtured your business, seen it stabilize and prosper, but as you examine the complexities of selling, you find that the hard work you've put in doesn't automatically translate to the value you expected. Why is it that, despite all the efforts and improvements, the anticipated offers do not materialize? I know. Not as epic as the opening to the previous chapter. I tried.

The truth hits hard. It took me a while to accept what I already thought may be possible, so the same might hold true for you. At the end of the day, working harder often doesn't mean your business value will shoot up. This realization can be disheartening, and in some ways downright depressing, because we sometimes don't know what else to do, but work hard, believing that each improvement will directly boost company value.

I assume you're reading this book because selling your business has crossed your mind, so let's play out that scenario. Last week, you decided to sell your business. You immediately started googling "how to sell your business." You found a ton of BS services and a few brokerage/listing sites and started going down the rabbit hole. This might have led you to this book—congrats! You found one actually written by a business owner just like you!

You step into the market filled with optimism. Maybe you contacted a broker, created a few high-level documents, and hit the market within a week only to face the reality that the offers are underwhelming—if they come at all. And then you start to blame yourself and wonder where you went wrong. Is it possible that preparation started too late? Was focus misplaced on aspects of the business that, while important, aren't the key drivers of value to an external buyer?

I've worked with many small business owners who struggled to attract serious offers. One of those businesses, a software development firm, had perfected their technology—a crucial aspect, indeed—but neglected to focus on how to present the business to potential buyers. What do I mean when I say potential buyers? Potential buyers are other small business owners, investment bankers, or CEOs, and usually come from a financial or operational background. Technology won't help these buyers understand the return on their investment. When planning on how to present this software development firm's value, we refocused the software firm's efforts on highlighting their robust customer acquisition strategy, and demonstrating their impressive recurring revenue model, both of which were key aspects that resonated with buyers. This shift in strategy transformed their market appeal, attracting offers that significantly exceeded the owner's expectations.

This experience underscores a critical lesson: the preparation for selling your business must align your business with market demands and buyer expectations. It's about understanding what makes your business attractive, not just to *you* but to the person who might take it to the next level. I'd almost go as far as to say that how *you* feel about the business may not be relevant at all to your exit strategy!

So, here's a key step. If you're contemplating selling your business, start by evaluating how buyers see your company. What stands out, and what might hold them back? Start by taking the **Exit Attractiveness Scorecard at ExitByFORCE.com/Weapons** to objectively assess your business's attractiveness from a buyer's perspective. The scorecard will be one of your Weapons to measure your progress as you prepare the business for an exit. Reflect on what aspects of a business catch your attention when you're in the buyer's shoes—are these elements evident and optimized in your own business?

As you move forward, think about how to position your business not just as a functional entity but as a potential gold mine for the right buyer. The effort you put into this strategic positioning can make the difference between a satisfactory exit and a truly lucrative one.

FORCE Exercise: Evaluate how buyers see your company.

- Who are we? What is our brand value?
- How are we known? Where is our thought leadership?
- What aspects might hold a buyer back?
- **Weapons: Take the Exit Attractiveness Scorecard located at ExitByFORCE.com/Weapons**

Notes:

MYTH 3: PLANNING FOR THE FUTURE CAN WAIT

Choosing to sell your business is one of the most significant decisions you'll ever make. It's not just a business transaction; it's a deeply personal and emotional journey. You've spent years, perhaps decades, building your business, and now you're contemplating passing it on to new ownership. This decision affects not only you but also your family, team members, and stakeholders.

You've likely done some research into succession and exit planning. Perhaps you've spoken to people in your network or brokers who've reached out in the past. But now, you're at a crossroads. Is selling the right choice for you and your family? Are you ready for the emotional and logistical challenges that come with such a monumental decision? Do you have an idea of what you want to do next?

The process can feel overwhelming. There are so many aspects to consider: financial, emotional, and practical. You might be wondering if you've thought of everything. Are you truly prepared to let go of something you've built from the ground up? Once sold, it's sold—there's no getting it back.

Honestly, half the battle is being in the right place at the right time and being fully prepared well in advance. You don't know when the opportunity will present itself, but sometimes you do have control, like when you put the business on the market. There are other ways to sell that can truly be rewarding. I sold both of my own businesses because the opportunity presented itself. The first business, we got taken advantage of, but the second one, we had planned to be ready. We were always ready, waiting, searching, and putting our feelers out in the market.

Like many businesses, there was so much more we could have done to increase our valuation with IT Trailblazers. Yes, we negotiated a fantastic multiple from a valuation standpoint, but we didn't even remove personal expenses that would have immediately increased EBITDA and exit valuation. One thing we did well was to split the office building, which we owned, into a separate LLC. This was done in advance so we could sell the office building as a real estate transaction and extract value from it. If we hadn't done this, a million dollars would have walked away when we sold the business because property doesn't get factored into EBITDA. With more time and without the stress of an exit "happening" to you, there is a lot that can be considered, a lot that can be saved, and more money to be made. There are so many things I wish we had done differently, and we could have done them if we had planned for it.

With ITTDigital, where I was the CEO, we were always well-positioned, and we weren't ever looking to actively exit the business. I was much more experienced with business exits, and wanted to always be ready for the right opportunity. I learned from my mistakes. We ran the business in a way that was desirable for acquirers. This gave us a seamless exit. We did not let the world happen to us; we controlled the journey and were ready when the opportunity presented itself. We Exited By FORCE!

Selling a business isn't about waiting around; it's about staging it for the future, much like a Jedi Master preparing for a decisive battle. (This is the only *Star Wars* metaphor I'm going to use. I promise!) Even if the time and place of a confrontation are unknown, the Jedi Master remains vigilant, honing skills and maintaining readiness through rigorous training. When the moment arrives, they execute flawlessly with unconscious competence. Similarly, keeping your business in peak condition means you're always ready to seize the right opportunity when it comes, not sitting around waiting for life to happen to you.

If you're still on the fence, take a look at the Exit Attractiveness Canvas, it's one of the Weapons in your arsenal. You can download the free **Exit Attractiveness Canvas by visiting ExitBy-FORCE.com/Weapons**. You don't have to fill it out line by line, but it will help get you thinking about the right topics and hopefully help you make a decision on timing. Maybe now is not the right time to start planning an exit, but it could be, and that's a decision only you can make. The Path You Choose Is Yours Alone.

This tool will guide you through the critical aspects of exit planning, helping you assess where you stand and where you want to be. It will assist you in identifying the gaps and preparing for the transition, ensuring that you're ready for whatever the future holds.

I hope by now you've realized the importance of starting early and being ready for whenever an opportunity presents itself. Of course, you are on a time line, and we are going to push that agenda forward, so all the more reason to be ready early.

Consider this book a road map for your journey. By the end of Episode 1, you'll have a clear picture of what your future holds and how to navigate the complexities of selling your business to Maximize Founder Value.

FORCE Exercise: Reflect on your reasons for picking up this book.

- What is your vision for life until you exit?
- Is there something motivating you to exit? What might that be?
- What are your fears about exiting? Is something holding you back?
- **Weapons: Start the Exit Attractiveness Canvas located at ExitByFORCE.com/Weapons**

Notes:

MYTH 4: JUST-IN-TIME EXIT PLANNING WORKS

Knowing the right time to start the exit process is never easy, but it's much harder to sell a business on a moment's notice. You may have endless reasons to sell right away, but they usually boil down to the same thing: the business has taken off and you want to cash in, the business has fallen and you're burned out, or there's been a life event that's changed your situation. These scenarios are very real to many business owners, and I hear them time and again—most never planned in advance to exit.

Sometimes, the idea of preparing for a sale can seem premature, yet being ready at any moment can be the difference between selling when you are ready with ease and waiting for years to exit or selling at a lower price point. You would be surprised by the number of founders that approach me with a medical condition or a change in life situation. It happens all the time—please don't think it cannot happen to you. Anyone above the age of fifty is prone to medical conditions. My grandma had a triple bypass heart surgery at fifty-four years old, and she didn't run a business. It happens all the time.

What happens to your business if you are unable to actively participate? You've built something amazing—can your number two, number three, or a family member take over in your absence? Doubtful. You're indispensable

I worked with a staffing company run by two men in their late sixties. Neither planned an exit strategy or succession plan; it was like they wanted to run the company forever. Even Warren Buffet has a plan for Berkshire Hathaway—he recently released his will, outlining how his three children, who have been groomed all their lives, will be fiduciaries for his estate.[4,5] Of course, he has billions, and the stakes are higher, but why shouldn't this be as important for us? Unfortunately, due to medical issues and life changes, the staffing company sold for $1 to one of my friends. My friend used the Exit By FORCE principles and sold the company a year later for over a million dollars.

Look, I get that you don't want to plan for these things, but life happens, and it can happen to anyone. It affects many people—not just you but your family, your employees, their families, etc. The business will collapse without you, and you cannot sell immediately, at least not for any significant value. You are becoming a desperate seller, which we touch upon in Episode 3.

Also, you miss out on opportunities that can arise unexpectedly. A strategic acquisition offer could come your way, potentially offering the most favorable terms for your life's work. However, if you're not prepared, you might let that opportunity slip by, losing out to an uncertain future. Being ready now means you can seriously consider any deal and position yourself to Maximize Founder Value.

IT Trailblazers, while we weren't ready to sell and had not planned for it, can be considered a Just-in-Time sale, and look what happened to us. The founder, my father, poured his life into it and involved many family members, including his children. We had a thriving business, and we didn't need to sell, but since the opportunity was too good to be true, we rushed into it. We didn't have time to educate ourselves, think about employment agreements or talk to others that have exited before, and learn about pitfalls. Instead, we pushed forward into the unknown. The experts on the other side, playing their own game, set out to deceive us from the very beginning—they were so professional that we didn't see it coming.

Also, how do you manage the transition process? We had employees that had been there for 20+ years, family members that would have to find new jobs, and pet projects across the organization. Sometimes, it's not about the money; it's about managing the transition for everyone involved, ensuring that team members could thrive under new ownership. In the end, we all lost—after all that work, we still ended up in a lawsuit because we tried to do it just-in-time.

For many, it's worse because they are physically unable to partake in the company, and it all goes to the dogs. Don't let your hard work waste away and your legacy disappear. Don't be that story of the man or woman who built an empire to watch it crumble away. Sometimes, that's why people sell for a dollar—at least they can say they sold and exited. Unfortunately, many companies fall into this category of selling for pennies. Do you really know what the companies around you sold for?

This experience underscores the importance of being prepared. Even if you're not ready to sell right now, it's crucial to position your business so that, in a worst-case scenario, you're all set. You can have someone step in and put it on the market or work with a professional to get it done for you. It's much easier.

Of course, preparing your business for a future sale takes time, effort, and money. You're busy with other priorities, and it might seem like too much work to set everything up now. On the other hand, think about the devastating downside if something happens. Wouldn't you rather be in a position to run the exit process from a boat in Mykonos? I would love that life. I could see myself on vacation on a catamaran and being like, "Hey, I'm done with this shit. Let's exit." And with the business already ready, it would be off to the races. No more heartache or frustration. Just forward momentum. It could be that easy, but not if you're trying to do it just-in-time.

The cost of procrastination is high, and the market waits for no one.

Is it worth being ready today for a future that may or may not come? Absolutely.

Again, The Path You Choose Is Yours Alone.

FORCE Exercise: Reflect on your stakeholders.

- Do you have other important stakeholders in the business such as partners, family, or friends?
- Are there any health conditions or life scenarios that you need to be prepared for?
- Can someone keep the lights on in your absence?

Notes:

MYTH 5: BUYERS WILL AUTOMATICALLY VALUE YOUR BUSINESS

Buyers want your business. They come in many forms: private equity firms, strategic acquirers, family offices, first-time entrepreneurs, and industry leaders. They see the potential in your company and are excited about growth through acquisitions. You have a wonderful business generating revenue and positive cash flows, making it a highly attractive target. To attract these buyers effectively, your business must be set up to showcase its value. Many businesses need proper staging from a buyer's perspective; they often lack the necessary systems and processes and carry too much risk when controls are concentrated with the owner.

The complication is that your business is not currently set up to attract buyers. Can you honestly tell me that if a potential buyer knocked on your door, you'd be ready to send out your data room, a repository of documents to showcase to a potential buyer, or at least your financials within

seconds? If so, that's a pretty good start. I hope anything you send off is cleaned up, well-staged, and demonstrates your value. If that checks out, can you prove to them that the business can run without you? If you can do that, stop reading, but more likely than not, you picked up this book to learn the hidden secrets, the magic, to Maximize Founder Value.

There are a few good tricks up ahead!

To make this simple, let's compare your small business exit to selling your house. You will see that I've used this metaphor throughout the book to simplify my explanations. You've built a wonderful home, filled with memories, and have enjoyed living in it for a long time. Great job on your beautiful design! The house is all yours; it has your great touches, your beliefs, and it has your quirks. Now, it's time to sell.

Let's think of a few actions you might take to sell your house. Yes, you might contact a broker, which I hope you haven't—they are virtually useless in the business exit world. We will touch more on this in Episode 3. You more than likely have to take care of some touch-ups, fix any broken tiles, make sure there are no leaks, and stage the house to attract a lot of attention in the market. Why would your business be any different? Similarly, your business needs to be well-staged to highlight its strengths and potential, making it irresistible to buyers.

Consider the scenario when you bought your first house. I'm sure you can relate to that. What about an investment house? Maybe you can relate to that too. I've bought a condo for investment, and, at a high level, the process for buying my current house didn't differ too much. You go online and search for houses; sometimes it comes through your network that someone is looking to sell.

You always keep a watchful eye on the houses you really want. You then take a look at the pictures of the staged house—known as financials for a small business. Well-staged financials make all the difference; we'll dive into this shortly. You then visit the house in person.

When you walk into the house, you have high expectations and want to be blown away. What happens when the house is under-whelming? The same goes for your business; you walk out the door, say bye-bye, and move on to the next. If the house is well-staged and gives you the wow effect, you start checking the water pressure, ask questions about the neighborhood, and check if everything was serviced/renewed/up-to-date. Does that change from a business? This is the operations part of the house. Can you see yourself living in this house? Can you see yourself running this business? Is it easy? Can it be done without the owner? Is it de-risked?

Finally, you check for everything else such as utility payments, foundation, HVAC, etc. You get an inspection done, called due diligence, and finally put in an offer. When looking at a business, you check resources—can they be maximized? You check for advanced features such as automation—can things be done without you? And finally, you check if the business can expand and grow and thrive with your investment and management. For some reason, buyers always feel they can do better than the entrepreneur, let's let them believe that! Stupid MBAs.

Selling a business is comparable to selling a home, with one crucial difference: in business you have the power to influence value significantly!

So put yourself in the buyer's shoes and prepare your business for sale. Buyers will not automatically see value in your business. They may be excited at the prospect of buying, think about it as an investment, or consider it as a bolt-on to grow. You need to cater the business to fulfill everything that a buyer could want and more. This should be their dream house.

Being prepared means having your house cleaned and staged before an opportunity arises. Some actions take time to manifest their full effect on your business, so starting now is essential. You need to transform your business into something that can be put on display, ensuring that every aspect is optimized and attractive to potential buyers. The process can seem daunting, with many actions to consider, and it's not always clear what should be done first.

The answer lies in the principles of Exit By FORCE. This book will guide you through refining your story and preparing your business to become a highly desirable acquisition target. Buyers want a great story—an engaging, authentic narrative about the purpose of your company and the journey you've taken to build it.

To achieve this, you need a structured approach. The Exit By FORCE principles provide a comprehensive framework to guide you through this process. This book will walk you through the specific actions and concepts you need to implement to be ready for any opportunity. By following these principles, you'll make your business the most desirable, efficient, and valuable entity in your industry. Acquirers will line up, eager to bid for your company, driving up its value.

When I was preparing ITTDigital for a potential sale, we meticulously transformed each aspect of the company using the FORCE framework. The results were unbelievable; I wished I had done it much earlier. A couple extra years with these principles in place and who knows where the business might have been. It was unrecognizable from where we started, and in a good way. When the opportunity presented itself, we were ready. Buyers saw the value immediately, and we were able to negotiate from a position of strength.

Your business has unique strengths that make it stand out. By showcasing these strengths and following the FORCE framework, you can transform your business into one of the most desirable, valuable, and efficient businesses to acquire in your industry. This approach doesn't require years of effort, luck, or hard work. It's about concentrating on the most impactful actions that make your company the most desirable option.

It's time to get your business well-staged for the fantastic exit you deserve. Let's dive into the FORCE principles and Exit By FORCE!

FORCE Exercise: Reflect on your ideal exit scenario.

- What does a successful exit look like to you? Do any specific requirements come to mind?
- Do you have any non-negotiables to do a deal?
- Have you thought about transition time as part of your vision?

Notes:

SUMMARY: THE JOURNEY BEGINS WITH YOU

You've embarked on a journey to prepare your business for a successful exit. By understanding the importance of readiness, reflecting on your business's unique strengths, and preparing to implement the FORCE principles, you're positioning yourself for a highly desirable and valuable exit.

When you look closely, you'll notice businesses across all industries adopting this strategy to position themselves as appealing acquisition targets and to secure exits on their own terms. This approach doesn't require years of effort, luck, or hard work. It's about concentrating on the most impactful actions that make your company the most desirable option within your industry.

As you continue with this book, you'll dive deeper into the FORCE principles—specific strategies and actions that will transform your business into one of the most attractive acquisition targets in your industry. This structured approach will guide you every step of the way, ensuring you Maximize Founder Value under the most favorable terms.

Take control of your exit strategy. Your journey to freedom begins now.

When the stakes are high, always be in control!

The Path You Choose Is Yours Alone!

FORCE Exercise: Reflect on the insights and strategies discussed in this Episode.

- Have your thoughts changed about taking control of your exit strategy?
- Are there simple steps you can start today to prepare for a successful exit?
- What are the biggest challenges or areas that you need help with?
- **Weapons: Finish the Exit Attractiveness Canvas located at ExitByFORCE.com/Weapons**

Notes:

2

TRUST IN THE FORCE

Navigating the complexities of exiting your business requires more than just knowledge—it demands a structured approach and unwavering confidence in your strategy.

In this episode, you'll delve into the FORCE methodology, a powerful framework designed to optimize your business for maximum value. By trusting in the FORCE, you'll transform your business into an irresistible acquisition target, ensuring you control the exit process and achieve the best possible outcome.

Embrace this journey with confidence, and let the FORCE guide you to a successful exit.

THE ART OF BECOMING AN ACQUISITION MAGNET

Buyers want to acquire to grow, and there are very few companies that fit their requirements. Your goal is to make them see *your* business as a "must-have" instead of a "nice-to-have." Buyers will come to the table with tough questions, probing into your financials, operational efficiencies, and overall risk. They do this to strengthen their bargaining position and justify lower offers. You're reading this book to take control of your journey and to get the buyer to change their mindset—to make them see your business as the turnkey solution they're looking for. We're going to convince them to buy your company at the highest possible price.

You might have noticed that only a handful of companies consistently get great opportunities. These are the attractive companies—the ones everyone talks about at conferences, the names that frequently come up in conversations. They always seem flush with business opportunities and are often the first to be considered for acquisition by larger competitors. These companies have the negotiating power to Maximize Founder Value under the most favorable terms.

The stark reality is that only one in ten businesses are acquired today.[6,7,8,] Most companies are not well-staged or positioned to attract buyers. They lack the necessary data and presentation to appeal to acquirers. When businesses that aren't properly staged go to the market, they often find themselves subjected to unfavorable terms and conditions yet are desperate to sell. They end up fighting for worthless opportunities.

Even if you are not currently an attractive business, you can turn it around. When the stakes are high, you need to take control; in other words, you need to Exit By FORCE. To stand out and command the best terms, your business must be impeccably staged and ready to impress at any moment. Potential buyers should see your company as an opportunity too good to pass up, not just another option in a crowded market. Once you start having conversations and showcase your staged business, more and more opportunities will follow. You will become the hottest house on the block by demonstrating professionalism, readiness, willingness for a deal, and timely communication, combined with an extremely well-run and well-positioned enterprise. What buyer could say no to that?

When I was growing ITTDigital, I made it a point to attend conferences and engage with as many people as possible. I saw every conversation as a potential partnership, even if they were with Hufflepuffs. One day, a typical conference-goer asked if I was open to an acquisition conversation and exploring potential synergies with his company. I was skeptical, not understanding the individual's credentials yet. I wasn't looking to actively exit and didn't want to waste any time, so I opened my laptop and opened up my acquisition documents, my staged house, my data room. I presented the numbers at a high level, explained the financial and operational house, and spoke about innovation and automation at the organization. We were a high-tech tech company. Surprisingly, the conference-goer jumped on it and other buyers caught wind. This was all only possible because I was ready to go; it was on my laptop, at my fingertips, and showcased my professionalism and willingness to do a deal.

It's similar to the story of Disney and Pixar. Pixar was originally the computer division of Lucasfilm; it was bought by Steve Jobs from George Lucas, and renamed Pixar.[9,10] At the time Disney was interested, Pixar wasn't actively looking to sell; they were doing fabulously well and were already a publicly traded company worth billions of dollars. However, after years of partnership, Disney's animation house was going down the tubes, and Bob Iger, newly appointed CEO of Disney, needed to do something drastic. He needed to make a statement to the world, and decided the animation studio was the place to start. Why build when you can buy? He worked with Steve Jobs to bring Pixar into the magic kingdom for $7.4 billion.[11] This example, while on a larger scale, perfectly illustrates the importance of being well-positioned all the time so that, when an attractive opportunity arises, you are in a position of power.

Always be ready, and always be in control! Trust in the FORCE.

FORCE Exercise: Reflect on your business before we jump into the FORCE framework.

- Can you think of anything that could be addressed to make your business attractive?
- Does something in your business give you a competitive edge, such as innovation or IP?
- How long will it take to be ready for an acquisition conversation?

Notes:

THE FORCE METHODOLOGY

Becoming an attractive business isn't as hard as it seems, and it certainly doesn't take years. It's not about perfecting your business; it's about making it extremely attractive in the buyer's eyes. So let's discuss the five key elements you need to have in place to Exit By FORCE:

Financial Optimization: Regardless of how great your product or service is, acquirers will struggle to recognize your value if your financial house isn't in order.

Operational Excellence: Acquirers will pay a premium for businesses that are easy to manage with minimal risk. This creates a compelling investor narrative.

Resource Maximization: Attractive businesses excel at doing more with less, maximizing output, minimizing waste, and improving profitability.

Cognitive Automation: Incorporating Artificial Intelligence (AI) and other automation techniques into your operations sets you apart and positions your company as a highly innovative tech play.

Expansion Dynamics: A strong digital presence, coupled with strategic partnerships and lead generation capabilities, positions you well. This gets you on the buyer's radar and makes you hard to resist.

Let's compare this to selling your house:

Financial Optimization: The staged house. Financials should narrate the story of the business. They should be well-organized, showcase value, cleaned up, and consistent. This is the first thing a buyer will see and must be flawless to create that "wow" effect. A single red flag could destroy credibility and trust, raising hundreds of questions we want to avoid. Many smaller companies don't even know about accrual-based accounting, so they don't know the true financial condition of their business. It must be perfect—it's the dream house.

Operational Excellence: This is everything within the house. The water pressure, appliances, electrical systems, plumbing, and

maintenance. This is the next big check when potential acquirers come for the second walk-around. This translates to organization chart, roles within the organization, system-driven process
management, and having all the necessary departments. Buyers
want to ensure that they can manage this business efficiently,
that everyone knows their job, and that they will get a return on
investment.

Resource Maximization: This is everything we need to run the
house. The dollar bills that go into maintaining operations, winning new business, and delivering to clients. Buyers will want
to see strategic resource allocation: neither bloat nor missed
opportunities. The efficiency of your decisions, as the owner
of a house or business, has a direct impact on the buyer's
impressions.

Cognitive Automation: This is the smart house. You walk in to the
sound of beautiful summer tunes, see the Roomba in cleaning
mode, the Nest with its perfect temperature, the lights dimmed
with the fading sunlight, and the fans automatically operating
to save on utilities. In your business, think about automation in
accounting, A/R, A/P, invoicing, follow-ups, payroll, taxes, IT support, data reporting, dashboards; really, throughout your business operations.

Expansion Dynamics: In a home, this can be a swimming pool,
a converted garage, or a mother-in-law suite in the basement.
For your business, this can be the sales pipeline, external presence, partnerships, and referral systems—anything that helps the
growth story continue and find the right buyers. These dynamics demonstrate your ability to bring on new clients or add new
family members to the business. It's the ability to see the future
empire from the building blocks!

This approach doesn't require years of effort, luck, or hard work. It's about focusing on the highest-value actions that make your company the most desirable option within your industry. These five steps are a powerful guide, which we will look at in great detail in this Episode.

The order is important. There's no point in jumping to automation when operations are not fully aligned. Automating the wrong parts of your business can be detrimental. Tesla, for example, initially struggled with over-automation and had to review each implementation, losing valuable time and money. They learned that some areas were better handled with a human touch.[12,13,14] We need to know how to apply technology effectively, starting from the top.

Similarly, if a house isn't staged properly—with the TV on the floor, the sofa not matching the coffee table, food stains on the counter, hair in the drains, and a scratched-up fridge with magnets haphazardly clinging to its sides—would you find it appealing? Or would you turn right around and find a house that appears loved and well-kept? Would you be able to put all of it aside to focus on aspects like water pressure? I think not. Potential buyers will be out the door in seconds. Let's get the financial house in order first before moving to operations or resources.

Once you have these five steps in place, the results will follow automatically. You will be amazed at the transformation. You will be introduced to buyers, clients, and influential people as the best-run company in your industry. Your clients and stakeholders will see a drastic improvement in service, leading to enhanced customer satisfaction and deeper relationships. They will work more closely with you, give you better terms, give you the benefit of the doubt, and willingly hand over millions of dollars. This is not magic. It's your ability to apply the FORCE framework that makes you hyper-resourceful and super attractive.

> The key is to concentrate on high-value actions using the latest and best industry practices while avoiding wastage in the trial-and-error process. Remember, 20% of your actions will determine 80% of your value. It's about focusing entirely on that crucial 20%.

"Your focus determines your reality."

– Qui-Gon Jinn, Jedi Master

We will start with the first part of the process, the staged house: Financial Optimization. When potential buyers ask about your business, the first question is, "Can you send me your financials for the last twelve months broken down by month and an overview of the last three years?" Now, it's game time.

If you haven't wielded the scorecard yet, now might be a good time to take out this Weapon and get your **Exit Attractiveness Score**—your starting point. As you apply these principles, your score will increase over time. You can swing a lightsaber as many times as you would like, just like you can take the scorecard as many times as you like—as the numbers improve, your confidence and trust in the process will increase.

Trust in the FORCE. You will see improvements, I promise! It will be a good measurement of where you are today and where you are tomorrow, showing how your hard work and efforts have paid off as you Exit By FORCE.

FORCE Exercise: Reflect on your current standing in each of the five FORCE areas.

- Have you heard of recent business exits? What do people say about them?
- Can you relate to the house metaphor? Do you agree with the thought process?
- Are there actions off the bat you could take to make the business run without you?
- **Weapons: Take the Exit Attractiveness Scorecard located at ExitByFORCE.com/Weapons**

Notes:

STEP 1: FINANCIAL OPTIMIZATION

Imagine walking into a beautifully staged house. Another house analogy, I know, but stick with me. Instantly, you're impressed by its cleanliness, organization, and charm. The careful selection of furniture and small touches help you envision what it might be like to live there. This first impression sets the tone for everything that follows. Similarly, when a potential acquirer looks at your business, your financials are their first impression. A well-organized, transparent, and robust financial setup will significantly enhance your business's appeal and value.

Your financials are the numeric story of your company's progress and performance over time. They detail how the business has performed, where it makes money, and where it spends money. A well-presented financial statement showcases the company's value proposition, ensuring it is fairly and consistently reflected and presented. This first impression can make or break your opportunity to command a high valuation.

No matter how innovative or successful your business is, if your financial house is not in order, acquirers will struggle to see its true value. This section is your guide to ensuring your financials are not just in order but optimized to reflect the best version of your business.

Revenue: The Lifeblood of Your Business[15,16,17]

Revenue is the lifeblood of your business, and how you present it matters. Consistent and clear revenue recognition methods are crucial. Highlight your stable revenue streams with long-term contracts and recurring revenue. This not only demonstrates stability, it assures buyers of the business's ongoing profitability.

Consider a comparison of Company Typical and Company FORCE. Both have the exact same financial numbers, but look closely at how they are presented. This example showcases a services-based company where the cost of goods sold is labor. This is exactly how I set up ITTDigital before its sale. These numbers are actual historic numbers of a business that worked with us in the past. It showcases a very real scenario.

Company Typical Revenue January - December 2023		Company FORCE Revenue January - December 2023	
	Total		**Total**
Income		Income	
Sales	$ 5,593,875.00	Fortune 500 Recurring Revenue	3,065,678.00
Total Income	$ 5,593,875.00	Fortune 2000 Recurring Revenue	1,532,839.00
		All Other Sales	976,149.75
		Interest Income	19,208.25
		Total Income	5,593,875.00

Company Typical depicts its sales in a single line item called Sales. Some organizations might break down multiple business lines, but it often ends up as Sales of Business Line X, Sales of Business Line Y, and Sales of Business Line Z, with additional lines for discounts and refunds. Here's the problem: when buyers look at this, they may not see the value of this revenue, leading to undervaluation due to perceived risk and instability. Why? The buyer might think, "This business has healthy revenues, but it must have small clients and it's going to be unstable if the owner leaves." At this stage, buyers are very conservative and look at businesses from a due diligence lens; that means they are trying to find fault with the business. Showing revenue in this setup creates a false impression that your business deals with small low-value clients. This is what we don't want to happen.

Here's another way to play it. **Company FORCE**, with the same revenue as Company Typical, shows a consistent revenue trend by accurately recognizing revenue for work done each month. Company FORCE further breaks down clients into valuable categories like Fortune 500 clients, Fortune 2000 Clients, and recurring revenue. This approach tells a compelling story of stability and professional management, making the business more attractive to potential buyers. Now the buyer might think, "Whoa, recurring revenue with top-name logos and high-end relationships. We need this addition to our business. With our combined capabilities and these deep relationships, we can blow these accounts wide open."

Check out the shift in mindset: the buyer is now convincing themselves to buy your company thanks to straightforward, simplistic changes like these. They recognize that the revenue should continue, the risk of the owner leaving is minimal, and the company consistently delivers to top-tier clients.

There are various ways to present your company in the best light and positively influence the buyer's narrative. Buyers typically approach acquisitions with caution and a risk-averse attitude; your job is to transform this perspective into one of urgency and desire. Show your business's value within the first thirty seconds of the buyer reviewing your financials. This might involve categorizing clients by size (large cap, medium cap, small cap) or by industry (life sciences, green energy, non-profit, federal/state contracts). The objective is for the buyer to immediately recognize that your business is a rare find worth pursuing. For this, you need to be able to articulate where your business is and where it can go—the greater POTENTIAL you can showcase, the greater the value in the mind of the buyer.

A crucial aspect of this is highlighting your company's value proposition and how the company continues to drive its own success. By emphasizing top-tier repeat customers and their loyalty, you validate your value proposition, demonstrating its strength and potential for growth post-sale. The buyer should feel that they are getting a steal and that the seller—you—might not fully understand the immense value you hold. Of course, you do know the value, and having read Exit By FORCE, you are ready to fully capture it.

Gross Margin Magic: Turning COGS into Gold

Company Typical
COGS + Gross Profit
January - December 2023

Cost of Goods Sold	
Cost of Sales	0.00
Total Cost of Goods Sold	$ 0.00
Gross Profit	$ 5,593,875.00

Company FORCE
COGS + Gross Profit
January - December 2023

Cost of Goods Sold		
Fortune 500 COGS	1,370,922.56	
Fortune 2000 COGS	831,058.31	
All Other COGS	626,383.23	
Interest Income	0.00	
Total Cost of Goods Sold	$ 2,828,364.10	
Gros Profit		% Gross Profit
Fortune 500 Recurring	1,694,755	55%
Fortune 2000 Recurring	701,781	46%
All Other Sales	349,767	36%
Interest Income	19,208	100%
Total Gross Profit	$ 2,765,510.90	

Let's move into the next critical aspect: Cost of Goods Sold (COGS). It's essential to accurately reflect this in your books—so if you need an accountant to get involved, get one. Gross profit matters immensely and is a vital consideration for potential buyers.

To present your business's profitability effectively, ensure all costs are correctly categorized under COGS. Separating variable costs from fixed costs offers a transparent view of your gross margin, helping potential buyers understand your actual cost structure and the true profit potential of your business.

Let's revisit the example of Company Typical and Company FORCE. Company Typical shows a COGS of zero. Does that mean the company has no costs associated with delivery? Many reading this book might argue that their main expense is labor, as they run a service-based business, and they have categorized it under labor. Here's the problem with this scenario. How do you (and your potential buyers) know what you're spending to achieve your revenue and whether you're actually profitable? I've seen this too many times, and it raises too many red flags. Once a buyer sees your COGS laid out like this, you will never be able to adequately convince them of your financial story. If it's not on paper, it doesn't count. It's all about credibility and building trust. Don't forget to consider other COGS such as materials, vendors, and other expenses; basically, anything directly involved in delivering the product or service.

Now, look at Company FORCE. Company FORCE accurately reports COGS for each revenue line item, allowing us to calculate the gross margin for each revenue type—whether by service line, industry, or client category. Depending on the situation, it may make sense for Company FORCE to break down revenue and COGS based on client groups. Or, it may make sense to list COGS based on service line or industry. The rule of thumb is that COGS must follow the breakdown of revenue so you should try multiple iterations of revenue and COGS combinations to find out what best suits your business to present it for an exit.

Looking at Company FORCE's books, you can see high gross margins within Fortune 500 clients, similar margins with Fortune 2000 clients, and slightly lower margins for other sales, such as smaller businesses or relationship-based sales. The buyer will understand why there are lower margins with small clients and appreciate the clarity this breakdown provides into high-value revenue streams.

> We don't include sales or management personnel in our COGS. They would be in a separate category in the next section of your books and do not impact gross margin. We don't want to undervalue ourselves by accidently including items in our COGS that don't necessarily belong. Other businesses on the market certainly won't. Ultimately, we are trying to sell our business, and this may require a bit of salesmanship!

It's imperative to determine the best way to break down COGS to create this success narrative for your company. To present a compelling gross margin some financial engineering or salesmanship may be necessary. The definition of salesmanship, if you didn't catch my drift, is slight strategic changes to portray a much better story. I'm sure you've done it to win clients, so let's do it to sell your business. Only do what you're comfortable with, as we still want to paint an honest picture. We're here to Exit By FORCE, not give away our business for pennies, so do what must be done!

FORCE Exercise: Reflect on your revenue and COGS break down.

- What is the financial story you want to tell?
- Do you have your delivery expenses tagged under COGS, including labor? Can a buyer easily evaluate Gross Margin?
- Can you think of another way to display your Revenue and COGS to make your company look better?

Notes:

Expense Alchemy: Transforming Chaos into Clarity

Company Typical General Expenses + Net Income January - December 2023		Company FORCE General Expenses + Net Income January - December 2023	
Expenses		**Expenses**	
6001 Sales	14,787.39	6000 Branding and Marketing	50,964.14
6002 Branding	7,265.32		
6003 Marketing	22,876.00	6010 Bank Charges & Fees	2,563.27
6004 Design	3,285.43	6020 Dues & subscriptions	37,685.00
6005 Website	2,750.00	6030 Rent & Lease	30,600.00
6010 Bank Charges & Fees	2,563.27	6035 Office Supplies & Expenses	18,821.79
6020 Insurance	10,000.00		
6021 Health Insurance	11,678.96	6040 Phone and Internet	5,476.73
6022 Dental Insurance	678.49	6050 Insurances	32,302.62
6023 Vision Insurance	135.47	6060 Legal & Professional Services	93,282.03
6024 Life and short term Insurance	3,231.20		
6025 BO, Cybertech, Workers Comp	6,363.95	6070 Meals & Entertainment	32,703.87
6027 Employee Insurance & Welfare	214.55		
6040 Dues & subscriptions	37,685.00	6080 Travel	84,174.50
6050 Accounting Fees	2,782.03	6085 Auto Expenses	11,883.39
6051 Legal Fees	29,000.00	6090 Client & Other Gifts	7,225.72
6052 Business Licenses	1,000.00	6100 Recruitment & HR	15,394.00
6053 M&A Expenses	60,000.00	6120 Training & Education	17,000.00
6054 Certification Fees	500.00	6140 Business Consultancy	729,270.06
6057 Books & Training	17,000.00	6200 Salary	846,004.47
6060 Office Supplies & Expenses	4,200.00	6250 Management Expenses	120,000.00
6061 Coffee & Snacks	2,438.00		
6062 Postage and Shipping	286.00	6300 Interest Paid	18,848.77
6063 Rent & Lease	30,600.00	6400 Taxes & Licenses	4,408.53
6064 Repairs & Maintenance	1,750.00	6500 Misc Expenses	1,179.00
6065 HOA Expenses	3,600.00	**Total Expenses**	**$2,159,787.89**
6066 Phone and Internet	5,476.73	**Net Operating Income**	**$ 605,723.01**
6067 Cleaning Services	3,600.00		
6070 Meals & Entertainment	32,703.87		
6080 Travel	84,174.50		
6082 Vehicle Lease	9,000.00		
6083 Auto Maintenance	800.48		
6084 Gas and Tolls	1,128.91		
6085 Auto Insurance	954.00		
6090 Utilities	2,947.79		
6100 Recruitment & HR	15,394.00		
6151 Business Consultancy	729,270.06		
6203 Sales Salary	349,103.24		
6204 Management Salary	259,677.73		
6205 Delivery Salary	2,151,153.82		
6207 Engineering Salary	137,038.70		
6209 Payroll Tax on Salary	202,788.14		
6217 Offshore Sales Salary	47,977.43		
6219 Offshore Support	526,629.51		
6254 Interest Paid	18,848.77		
6256 Taxes & Licenses	4,408.53		
6260 Client Gifts	7,225.72		
6280 Management Expenses	120,000.00		
6300 Misc Expenses	1,179.00		
Total Expenses	**$4,988,151.99**		
Net Operating Income	**$ 605,723.01**		

Since we're in the era of scrolling, let's scroll to the bottom of these financial books, where general expenses can be found. The goal for this section is simplicity. Think about what you might look for when analyzing the general expenses of a potential company you'd like to purchase. Likelier than not, a buyer is analyzing how well a company-for-sale has been running and whether it's been able to keep costs in check. However, you also want buyers to see potential areas for cost reduction. If the business appears to be running too lean, it might raise concerns about the buyer's ability to achieve greater returns on their investment.

Buyers want to purchase companies where they can identify ways to operate more efficiently. This foreshadows an increase in profits and, therefore, an increase in company value after purchase. They will also look for ways to reduce or merge expenses with the current operations of their existing company to reduce combined expenses and increase combined profits. Your goal is to strike a balance.

Looks like it's getting typical to compare Company Typical and Company FORCE. Dad joke.

Where Company FORCE has only a few line items, Company Typical's financials show numerous accounting categories called general ledgers. Company Typical has broken out sales, marketing, branding, design, and website expenses as separate line items, each showing small, questionable amounts. Similarly, accounting, legal, business licenses, M&A fees, and certification fees are listed as individual categories. These are broken down too much. Detailed accounting is by no means wrong—you should know what you're spending money on—but your buyers simply don't need this much information, so keep it out of the staged house. In this case, less is more. You don't want buyers to ask too many questions like, "Why are they spending so much on legal fees? Is there a pending lawsuit?" or "What exactly are business licenses and certification fees? Is there something we don't understand?"

Instead, consolidate these expenses. One line could be called Branding and Marketing, and another could be Professional Expenses or Legal and Professional Fees. When you group expenses under broader categories, they appear more straight-forward and reasonable. For instance, Legal and Professional Fees can encompass legal, incorporation, accountant, tax filing, certifications, and other business expenses. Grouping expenses under broader categories makes it easier for buyers to skim over the line without raising unnecessary flags or drawing attention to the wrong things.

> Here are some more examples of too much detail. Items like Coffee and Snacks, Postage and Shipping, Maintenance Work, HOA Fees, and Cleaning Services can be consolidated into a single category called Office Supplies & Expenses. Similarly, for Vehicle Lease, Auto Maintenance, Tolls, and Gas, group them into Auto Expenses. Make it simple!

We want to present expenses as appropriate, reasonable, and consistent. The buyer should be able to scan this section quickly and move on. Hopefully, the buyer is coming up with a few cost-cutting improvements while glazing over these numbers, and their work is made easier when the dollar amounts in each cat-egory are larger. They might also start thinking about consoli-dation with their current operations and how to increase the combined business valuation post acquisition. This is exactly what we want them to do! Remember, they will ask for a monthly breakdown of the last twelve months, so make sure it looks clean and consistent!

Expense Detox: Personal Costs Be Gone!

Company FORCE
Personal Expenses Included
January - December 2023

Expenses	Included	Removed	Personal Expenses	Description
6000 Branding and Marketing	50,964.14	50,964.14	0.00	
6010 Bank Charges & Fees	2,563.27	2,563.27	0.00	
6020 Dues & subscriptions	37,685.00	25,689.23	11,995.77	Subscriptions: Netflix, Spotify, etc
6030 Rent & Lease	30,600.00	30,600.00	0.00	
6035 Office Supplies & Expenses	18,821.79	12,821.79	6,000.00	Home Office Rebuild
6040 Phone and Internet	5,476.73	1,963.00	3,513.73	Family Cell Phone + Home Internet
6050 Insurances	32,302.62	29,381.33	2,921.29	Parents Medical Benefits
6060 Legal & Professional Services	93,282.03	69,471.12	23,810.91	Personal Taxes & Visa/Legal Expenses
6070 Meals & Entertainment	32,703.87	18,486.23	14,217.64	Personal Meals & Entertainment
6080 Travel	84,174.50	44,698.46	39,476.04	Personal Travel
6085 Auto Expenses	11,883.39	0.00	11,883.39	Personal Auto
6090 Client & Other Gifts	7,225.72	7,225.72	0.00	
6100 Recruitment & HR	15,394.00	15,394.00	0.00	
6120 Training & Education	17,000.00	3,500.00	13,500.00	Family Education and Classes
6140 Business Consultancy	729,270.06	729,270.06	0.00	
6200 Salary	846,004.47	846,004.47	0.00	
6250 Management Expenses	120,000.00	0.00	120,000.00	Transfer to Family LLC
6300 Interest Paid	18,848.77	18,848.77	0.00	
6400 Taxes & Licenses	4,408.53	4,408.53	0.00	
6500 Misc Expenses	1,179.00	1,179.00	0.00	
Total Expenses	$2,159,787.89	$1,912,469.12	$247,318.77	Total Personal Expenses
Net Operating Income	$ 605,723.01	$ 853,041.78		

Company FORCE
Personal Expenses Removed
January - December 2023

	Included	Removed	Valuation Difference
4X EBITDA	$2,422,892.02	$3,412,167.12	$989,275.10
6X EBITDA	$3,634,338.03	$5,118,250.68	$1,483,912.65
8X EBITDA	$4,845,784.05	$6,824,334.24	$1,978,550.19
10X EBITDA	$6,057,230.06	$8,530,417.80	$2,473,187.74

You've set up your general ledger and consolidated categories, so now lets evaluate all expenses going through the business. Are there expenses we should stop putting on the company? It's not uncommon for business owners to reduce their tax burden by running some personal expenses through the business. This might include the family cell phone bill, auto expenses, internet and home office costs, subscriptions like music, TV, magazines, news, gym services, and other miscellaneous expenses such as insurance, travel, ride-sharing, and restaurant bills. However, as we're looking to sell, it's crucial to ensure that all personal expenses are properly removed from the business accounts.

I've seen owners go as far as removing actual business expenses to drive up valuation. In the end, you're getting a multiple of EBITDA; so the better the EBITDA, the more galleons coming your way.

Let's assume your monthly personal expenses total $10,000. This amount per month equates to $120,000 per year, and at a 10X valuation, that's a whopping $1.2 million you flushed down the drain. I don't know about you, but that's a lot of Versace toilet paper. Owners shortchange themselves millions of dollars by not removing these expenses from their business before a sale, especially your vehicle—please remove it; no one wants it.

Personal expenses can raise questions during the sale process. Some advisors may suggest an "add-back" or a line item adding them back and calling it personal expenses. But ask yourself, if you were buying the business, would you accept these "add-backs" as personal expenses and pay an additional million dollars for the company? Likely not! You're going to negotiate tooth and nail over those expenses. Add-backs destroy trust and could kill the deal. Even if the buyer doesn't say anything about these expenses, they will absolutely decrease the offer to get back to the same value as if the expenses were considered against EBITDA.

Don't get caught in this trap—it creates mistrust and unnecessary complications. This is a multimillion-dollar deal, and fighting over a few thousand dollars of expenses is counterproductive.

The cardinal rule is to remove all personal expenses at least six months in advance. Yes, that could mean paying higher taxes, but don't be penny wise and pound foolish. Clean up the books, remove personal expenses, demonstrate a healthy EBITDA margin, and create the necessary wow effect.

FORCE Exercise: Reflect on General and Personal Expenses.

- Are your personal expenses and business expenses separate, clear, and concise?
- Can you list all the Personal Expenses running through the business?
- How do you feel about the breakdown of your General Expenses? Do you see any flags?

Notes:

EBITDA Magic: Balancing the Lean and the Dream

Earnings Before Interest, Taxes, Depreciation, and Amortization (EBITDA) is a key metric for evaluating business profitability. To enhance your EBITDA, focus on reducing unnecessary expenses and optimizing operational efficiency. Presenting a strong EBITDA in your financial statements can significantly boost your business's attractiveness to buyers. However, it's essential to strike a balance between running lean and showcasing an organization that's investing in future growth.

While a lean operation can enhance EBITDA in the short term, demonstrating strategic investments in people and growth initiatives shows buyers that your company is well-positioned for sustained success. In future chapters, we'll explore how targeted investments in key areas can drive growth and further enhance your business's value while maintaining Financial Optimization.

Being proactive on EBITDA management a couple of years in advance of an exit event can make the Exit By FORCE method even more valuable. It ensures that when the time comes to sell, your business is in the best possible shape to Maximize Founder Value.

Financial Pulse: Managing Working Capital Wisely

Now that we have the first impression taken care of, let's continue down this rabbit hole into financial operations. Financial operations are the day-to-day financial activities that must be done to run the business successfully. These actions affect cash flows and working capital requirements. Our goals are aligned; we want you to keep as much money as you can from the deal, so let's take action accordingly.

Working capital is the amount of money the business needs to run its operations successfully. This amount can be calculated by the difference between accounts receivable (AR) and Accounts Payable (AP) and is usually considered the business's property. That means it will directly impact our take-home cash; the higher the working capital requirement, the less we take home from the deal. Buyers won't bring this up during the initial negotiations, but will insist that a few months' worth of cash reserves stay with the business at closing. It's always added at the last minute and easily justified by the buyer. We need to figure out how to reduce working capital to the best of our ability.

For example, your Fortune 2000 clients have ninety-day payment terms, and you need enough cash or a working line of credit to bridge the gap between operations (AP) and payments (AR). All of my enterprise clients have ninety-day payment terms—it's extremely difficult to deal with, but we want their business and our margins should justify this. During times of low interest rates, take out the line of credit and use it as a tax write-off; it was almost like free money in 2020. In 2024, interest rates are the highest they've been in decades, and I'm only using my cash reserves because the cost of borrowing money is too expensive.[18,19] I hope you've saved up cash reserves instead of distributing all your profits. Either way, evaluate the best option for you based on your business circumstances.

Working capital is owned by the business. As business owners, we want to reduce the working capital requirement before selling, which means decreasing the time to receive payment and increasing the time to release payment. Keep your dollars as close to you as you can. Here are a few steps to achieve this.

The Receivables–Payables Dance: Cash Flow Control

Efficient management of accounts receivable (AR) and Accounts Payable (AP) is critical. Too often, businesses invoice late and collect payments after the terms have expired. Have you ever delivered a project and forgot to invoice the last three milestones, or had your executive assistant fall sick, so all your invoices are delayed? I've never let this happen! I once outsourced a portion of a big pharma contract to an e-learning supplier to manage our internal workload. The supplier forgot to invoice $60,000 worth of work; they sent us the invoice six months later without invoicing any of the milestones in-between. While I paid them for their services, another company could have easily ignored this invoice.

Take care of yourself and your money; always be in control when the stakes are high. It's tough to have money conversations and it's even harder to collect on the cash.

Start by scheduling a bi-weekly meeting with your finance team or executive assistant to review AR and invoicing. During these meetings, ensure that everything that can be invoiced is invoiced promptly. Remember, most payment terms start from the time of invoicing, not when the work is done, so invoice as early as you can. Many project management (PM) and billing systems can assist in automating these processes. Find the best software for your type of business to ensure you never miss a beat. I've used QuickBooks for my businesses. Anything recurring should be automated and sent out without manual intervention.

Cash is king, and collecting money is your most important job. However, always play the good guy and let a team member be the bad guy who follows up and collects payments. Your first line of defense is the fully automated system that should invoice clients and send reminders for upcoming or overdue payments.

If that doesn't work, assign a team member to consistently badger the client's accounts payable team until payments are made. This means everything: call, text, LinkedIn message, email—anything you can do to get in touch with the payer. For invoices delayed beyond ninety days, more stringent actions should be taken. My team usually writes a friendly message to stop service—this usually resolves the issue for anything ongoing or mission-critical. If that doesn't work, I, myself, call the client or visit them and try to put a positive twist on it, asking if they need help or if there is something preventing payment release. If there is an extenuating circumstance, your goodwill can go a long way to maintaining a business relationship and establishing your credibility and respect in your industry. If the good act doesn't work, stop service and send a legal notice on the default of payment. I know this is hard, but a client is not a client if they don't pay for the service, and buyers will straight-up disregard any delayed payment over thirty days. Boom! Right off your top line.

Sometimes, bringing in an external entity like Kenobi Capital can expedite this process. Clients take external agencies more seriously, knowing they mean business and will represent your interests rigorously. An external agency can also be a lot harsher without ruining your personal or professional relationships. I've used this tactic multiple times, and it usually works.

Last, consider incentivization schemes to induce clients to pay early. Although most large clients have rigid processes, offering 1–2% discounts for payments within ten days can work. Many clients seriously consider discounts because they have to report it on their corporate books. Sometimes it may be advantageous to them to pay early. Sometimes they will outright reject it, but we still need to try and reduce working capital requirements by reducing our outstanding accounts receivable. Nothing ventured, nothing gained. You never know when a client will come back and request such an arrangement. In many cases, clients will have a third-party service pay you in advance for a percentage of the invoice. It might make sense depending on the situation.

Pro tip, and this is my favorite! Close to the end of the year, offer clients the ability to "park" money with you if they haven't used their budgets. I usually have this conversation in person. Remember, your client counterparts report into their corporate overlords, and these overlords control the budget, which means your client counterparts must relinquish any unused funds to them. Your client counterparts, the team that works with you, will lose the current budget and most likely get a reduced budget the following year since they didn't use it up! You'd be surprised how many millions of dollars you can receive in advance. At one point, I had to pay taxes on $2.5 million of advance payments. Of course, the tax accountant deferred the tax obligation. (This is why I strongly recommend working with an accountant!) Still, this reduces payment terms to zero and lowers working capital requirements with a promise of guaranteed business. Does it get any better? And trust me, you're not giving that money back—ever. I didn't, even when the client didn't give us enough new business to realize it.

Payables Mastery: Working with Suppliers

On the other end of the spectrum is accounts payable. We have vendors and partners supporting our operations, and we need to extend our payment terms without causing too much friction. It should be done in a way that they don't put up a fight and trust that they will be paid. It's a fine line.

While never paying a credit card late is a cardinal rule, let's explore ways to extend payment terms with other vendors. In your business, you might rely on smaller companies that you outsource work to, as well as professional services such as accountants, insurance, and legal services. While you can't delay payments for essential supplies like building materials or employee salaries, you should focus on pushing the rest out.

Let me tell you a story on how I learned to do this. At ITTDigital, I had a team of six people doing work for an intermediate company providing services to the state of New York. New York state pays in thirty days—I knew this, and my client knew this. I had six people on this project, yet the vendor would pay me, on schedule, sixty days after an invoice was sent. I used to get super frustrated; we threatened late fees and removing our team, but I couldn't do anything. Was I really going to lose six people billing on time and materials on a project because of payment delays? Hell no! So what did I do? I sucked it up, stopped following up, and the payment came in consistently at the sixty-day mark. Eventually, I let it go and considered it a cost of doing business. That's how I learned this strategy: one of my clients did it to me, and I replicated it across outgoing payments.

Yes, there were initial frustrated emails from my suppliers; the accounts payable team and my executive assistant took the brunt of it. We set up a scheduling platform and provided screenshots of the scheduled payment, and lo and behold, suppliers received the money on the date promised. We moved payment terms from thirty days to forty-five days, then to sixty days, and some were even fine with ninety days. And that's how you extend outbound payments, increase accounts payable, and reduce working capital requirements!

If you are consistent, show proof of payment, and never destroy trust, it will all work out. Again, if a vendor asks for payment details, your executive assistant can provide a screenshot showing that the payment is scheduled and approved, waiting to be executed. It's a game—make sure you're playing it and driving your agenda.

> We automated many aspects of this. The payment scheduling tool would communicate at variable intervals when payments were scheduled to be sent and when payments were actually sent. This also made internal processes easier: my executive assistant (EA) would put the invoice in the system; sometimes vendors would email the invoice directly to the system. It goes through the platform, and I approve all payments once a week, but my EA would schedule them out as far as possible. It worked seamlessly. Automation was key as it removed all emotion from this process. You don't need to think about sending manual emails or how to start the conversation that could turn into a confrontation. I've used a few tools, and currently, I'm using Brex to manage money and payments.

These techniques are standard business practices that will help reduce working capital requirements, improve your balance sheet, and make you more attractive to buyers. They will be impressed by your company's ability to manage cash flows and maintain healthy client and vendor relationships. Implementing these processes will significantly add value to your business, and at the very least, reduce working capital requirements so more money ends up with you.

FORCE Exercise: Reflect on your working capital requirements.

- Have you invoiced everything that needs to be invoiced? Are you 100% sure?
- How does your accounts receivable summary report look? Any payment delayed over thirty days, sixty days, or ninety days? What aggressive actions can be taken to recover funds?
- What is the approval process for money leaving the company? Do you have a system in place to push out payment terms?

Notes:

Money in Motion: Capital Management Essentials

Now that you've staged your business, reduced personal expenses, increased gross margin and EBITDA, collected outstanding payments, and decreased working capital requirements, you might be wondering how much more there can be!

I'm an investment buff, so let me give you something to think about that most M&A folks won't know to tell you! Business owners tend to be focused on their business to such a degree that management of excess cash may not be in their purview. But this is the wrong way to approach it. There are many aspects to Financial Optimization, but for this last crucial section, let's talk about putting your money to work.

If you have extra cash, or managed to score a loan at a cheap fixed interest rate relative to current market, you're PRIMED to reap an additional benefit on that extra cash. At the time of writing this book in 2024, business loan interest rates have soared between 8% to 12%, making it wise to pay off any lines of credit to reduce interest expenses and invest any excess cash so it's working for you.[20,21] Of course, if you have a fixed SBA (Small Businesses Administration) loan at 2.5% or any other fixed interested rate debt under 5%, which is extremely low in today's market, keep it! The big advantage here is that we can invest any extra funds to earn a rate of return higher than the fixed interest rate and profit on the difference!

Consider the story of a client of mine who had $2 million sitting idle in a regular JPMC checking account. She didn't need the money for daily operations and didn't want to withdraw it from the business. We moved this money to an investment vehicle yielding 5%, which allowed her to generate $50,000 per year just in interest income. At a 10X valuation, that interest income added $500,000 to the business's value at exit. She not only earned the interest, but also earned 25% extra on idle cash and distributed the $2 million plus interest to herself when the business sold. That's a win-win-win scenario!

I've seen business owners make the mistake of allowing excess cash to be part of the deal and paid later. Don't let this happen. $2 million is a lot of money! When the stakes are this high, always be in control.

Whether you're a small business or a large one, it's really important to figure out how money can make you more money, regardless of exiting. Apple has an entire team dedicated just to managing excess cash; of course, it's in the billions of dollars, but the effort and thought process is there![22,23] You need to figure out how to do this as well. Here are some options: in 2024, safe money market funds like VMFXX yield above 5%, many banks offer 5%+ for deposits, and equity premium income funds such as JEPI are becoming increasingly popular.[24,25] That means any idle cash should be generating a return for the business and for your personal finances.

For each $100,000 in a normal bank account such as JPMC or BOA, you are leaving $5,000 on the table ($100,000*5%). That's like paying the bank $400 per month for an account. Business accounts keep a lot of excessive cash, so the money adds up! I don't know about you, but I don't like to give my hard-earned money away to banks. They are pretty much investing your deposits and taking the return for themselves. Consider platforms like Brex, which provide yield on any cash balance in your checking account, generating daily interest on unused funds. This approach helps you maximize your cash value without locking it up in long-term investments.

This is important! Make sure your money is working for you. This landscape might change, so it's crucial to evaluate the best investment options available to you. **Feel free to review the cash management portfolio and other resources at ExitByFORCE.com/Weapons or reach out so we can advise you based on the current market.**

FORCE Exercise: Reflect on your extra cash.

- How much money do you need in your business account and personal account to be comfortable with upcoming expenses?
- Are you currently investing your idle business cash to generate interest income?
- What is your money management philosophy?
- **Weapons: Implement the cash management portfolio located at ExitByFORCE.com/Weapons**

Notes:

Financial House

While these high-value actions conclude our discussion on Financial Optimization, there are many more facets to consider, especially when selling your business. One such example is creating an M&A data room, a repository to share with potential buyers, almost instantly. You can find a lot of information on data rooms online. At a bare minimum ensure you have three years' worth of financials, details on top clients by revenue and industry, documentation for any balance sheet investments or liabilities, and forecasted growth over the next three to five years.

Focus on the key aspects above and get your financial house in order. These processes take time to show results, and buyers will want to see the last twelve months of your books. The earlier you implement these steps, the better. Sometimes, presenting the last six months as optimized financials can work, especially if a new CFO joined or external counsel changed operations. A firm like Kenobi Capital can help convince buyers accordingly, nudging them into what they already perceive, that you are a fantastic company to acquire.

In this section, we've covered critical aspects of Financial Optimization. By implementing these strategies, you ensure that your business is financially attractive and ready to command the highest possible value. Remember, the first impression is everything, and a well-staged financial house can significantly enhance your business's appeal to potential acquirers.

Considering my background, it's probably no surprise that I was extremely prepared when an opportunity arose to sell ITTDigital. I had the financial house in order with a well-prepared data room, and even at the first conversation, I was able to share key information with potential buyers that impressed them right off the bat. Not only did I have my financials in order, but having them prepped allowed me to speak about it in an elevated, crisp fashion that made ITTDigital look irresistible. This preparation paid off when the potential buyer saw a clear, profitable, and well-managed business, leading to a successful and lucrative exit.

Your business can achieve the same results by following these steps. Financial optimization is not just about numbers; it's about presenting the best version of your business to attract and impress potential buyers. The next step in your journey is Operational Excellence.

Let's Exit By FORCE!

FORCE Exercise: Reflect on your financial house.

- How do you feel about Financial Optimization within your business?

- Do you think you are ready to provide a buyer with all the staged information needed to Maximize Founder Value?

- What is your game plan to execute the strategy and steps listed above?

- **Weapons: Review the Financial Optimization Checklist in the Exit By FORCE Toolkit located at ExitByFORCE.com/Weapons**

Notes:

STEP 2: OPERATIONAL EXCELLENCE

Beyond the initial charm of your potential house, the potential next homeowner starts to check the plumbing, electrical systems, and appliances. Each detail, from the water pressure to the condition of the washer and dryer, contributes to the house's overall value and desirability. Similarly, when potential buyers evaluate your business, they look closely at your operational systems and processes.

Achieving Operational Excellence is the next critical step after Financial Optimization. While financials provide a snapshot of your business's health, your operations validate these numbers, building confidence in buyers that your business is well-managed and sustainable with systems and processes in place. Operational Excellence demonstrates that your business is not only profitable but also efficient, scalable, and capable of maintaining high performance under new ownership.

Systems, Systems, and Systems[26,27,28]

Systems are the key to de-risking the most important person in the business—you. Your hard work, prowess, bravery, and risk-taking have taken the company from zero to one. You are now running a multimillion-dollar enterprise, having learned every aspect of it by living it. You know every detail from people to technology to client relationships to service providers. You are the most crucial asset to your business. Now, as you look to move on and extract value from your creation, what is your organization valued without its most important player? Without systems and processes, not much, and that's why we need to focus on this!

If you have been running a well-organized business, you may have implemented a customer relationship management (CRM) system, project and resource management tool, and core business function tools. Many businesses grow upward of $25 million through the sheer willpower and intelligence of the owner, but this doesn't hold up when you are looking to exit. It's essential to have these tools in place so you can present the current business standing and ensure a new management team can take over during the transition period. These systems, when implemented and managed correctly, will provide vital data to elevate the business valuation. It's all about the numbers!

Imagine a buyer looking at your business without these systems in place. What would you ask a business owner if you wanted to acquire their company? The buyer might be thinking, "This business looks fantastic, but the owner seems heavily involved in operations. I'm worried that clients might walk away after the owner leaves. How do I verify client relationships, ensure contracts are professional and renewed, and assure the company's ability to win new business and grow in the long run?" Or "How do I know this business is profitable across projects and if customers are delighted by our services and delivery? If only there was a way to review a few projects and understand if the company is operating well." Don't be insulted by this thought process. This is not to say that these are issues in the business or actions are not being done properly, it's to think about the buyer's perception and how to address it.

These are important questions and every buyer is thinking about them, so let's address them head-on and create another layer of trust to make this deal happen. There are two critical tools you need in order to show a buyer your worth: a CRM and a PM tool. Let's get into it.

From Contacts to Connections: The CRM Advantage[29,30]

A Customer Relationship Management (CRM) system is an important tool and generally one of the more expensive software solutions that a business uses. This is because sales teams usually have higher budgets than their cost-cutting delivery counterparts.

Deploy a cost-effective CRM system across the organization to track and analyze all customer interactions. A CRM system like HubSpot or Salesforce can help you manage client relationships comprehensively, ensuring all deals and interactions are recorded. This helps you track your upcoming pipeline accurately, giving potential buyers confidence in your sales process. If you already have a tool you love that's implemented and the entire team is using it, it's best that you keep that tool. On the other hand, if you don't have anything in place or the tool is outdated, consider using something new, that might have more advanced features. Each business is different, so it's important to select the right software for your business, but it's also important to choose something that is well-known in the market, as opposed to a small, random CRM system. It also helps them skim over reports as needed.

HubSpot is free, so if you don't have anything in place, that's a great place to start. At ITTDigital we used Zoho CRM and HubSpot. Most CRM systems have very similar features, the question is: how robust of a management tool do you need? That will give you your starting point.

> The importance of a CRM tool is to clearly display client relationships through interactions, communication, events, personnel profiles, and won/lost business. All of this falls under the term activity. The more activity you have, the better. The most important aspect of any CRM system is always keeping it up-to-date. While having a CRM system for your business is generally good practice, as business owners, we usually ask our teams to track the most important aspects and move on. We may not add specific information about client contacts or discussions around payment terms and parking money, or even the number of proposals submitted that are won and lost. Usually, we just add proposals submitted and won business; while important, this is very basic, and doesn't showcase the deep relationships we have with our clients.

Here, our goal is to convince a buyer that we are on top of our game and that the BUSINESS has deep relationships, not just the owner. We should ensure that the last six months of data is accurately represented with a lot of activity from our sales teams. Anyone interacting with a client should have access to the CRM and record it. A lot of times we forget to include our delivery heads or project managers, but these folks have a ton of inside information from working on projects. Also, client teams let their guard down around delivery team members because they aren't in active negotiation with them. Make sure you collect these insights and include them in the CRM process.

Once our CRM system is in place and we have set it up for the buyer's consumption, we should get the entire sales team to use the system in the exact same way. This might require a few workshops and training events along with a few audits to drive it home. People don't like change, so have your executive assistant speak to those who do not follow the process. Praise in public and punish in private. At any instance, we should be able to bring out a report on pipeline, submitted proposals, forecasted revenue, win ratio, and revenue in progress. These are all questions the buyer will ask and we need to answer with confidence.

Once everyone is on the same page, instruct your sales head and the sales team to write a standard operating procedure (SOP) for how your business uses the systems. Use ChatGPT to speed up the process, edit and format the document, and let's get it added to your new Operations Handbook for the business.

Tools of the Trade: Project and Resource Management[31,32]

A project management (PM) tool will give you a clear picture of how efficiently your team is delivering on each project and across projects. For the purposes of selling the business, you want to show the incoming buyer that your business is run professionally and that you can track and measure how well you are doing on each engagement. Basically, is delivery on time and on budget. I'm sure you've used that phrase before!

Project management for services businesses is simple: the business charges the client a certain amount of money, and needs to maintain a specific margin, thus, the team must deliver the project within a very specific budget and timeline. At ITTDigital, when we submitted a proposal for $250,000, we aimed for a minimum margin of 40%, so our maximum delivery budget was $150,000. We got to the price point by estimating the cost of each resource and the effort needed on the project. We can use this effort estimate breakdown to understand where each project stands from a cost and time line perspective, and to be able to showcase this to the buyer. Honestly, this report should be created to make decisions internally; it's a fantastic report. The added benefit is that it helps address all the buyer's delivery doubts.

You should be able to create projects within the PM system which include an effort estimate for each skill type on the project. Then you can add your hourly estimated cost for that skill type, and have your team track the progress and time line on the PM system. Regardless of the business you are running, ensure you can track total costs, efforts, and time line. At ITTDigital, I used a tool called OpenProjects where we onboarded 200+ users for free. It might be a good place to start if it fits your business. You need to know the actual profitability at a project, client, and team level. This data is crucial and buyers will ask for it. Once this is in place, it's important that we follow the same steps that we did for the CRM system.

As with a CRM system, a project management tool is only useful if it's updated daily. Otherwise, the data becomes inconclusive. If your business already has a tool in place, fantastic. Ensure that it's up-to-date and the workforce is trained and in compliance with the tool. If not, get one implemented quickly and backdate it for about three months so you have a baseline working process. Over the next few months, continue to monitor the system, perfect the process with your learnings, and create an SOP that goes into your Operations Handbook.

With a streamlined system in place, you should be able to provide your buyers with real-time reports on the status of your business. Sometimes, negotiations can go on for a few months, and you may need to be ready with the updated history. Buyers can tell when information is out of date, and this will hurt credibility. It's better to have the latest and greatest information at your fingertips and update your data room, the document repository of our staged business, monthly.

There will always be questions when a buyer digs into your operations because you have created the business to your liking; you've lived in the house. They might see other ways of doing things, which are perfectly acceptable. You should ensure you can justify logic with data and showcase that to the buyer. This should resolve any question they may have and it's up to them what the business looks like post transaction. Keep the discussion to the company's ability to deliver, why some projects may/may not be delayed or over budget, and the improvements you make every day to strive for a more efficient business. Ensure you have a project status report, profitability or cost-to-budget report, resource utilization report, and a customer satisfaction report (nice to have). This shows a well-run business that's able to make decisions quickly. It will also help the buyer make a decision faster.

So let's recap—buyers are already interested because they've seen your well-laid-out financials. Now they can take a look at your CRM system to see a fantastic pipeline, and peek into your PM tool to get information about productivity, profit margins, and overall delivery. There's no two ways about it at this point—buyers now know exactly how valuable you are.

FORCE Exercise: Reflect on these two core systems.

- What is the shape of your CRM system at this time and is there any room for improvement?
- How do you use your PM tool to improve the operations of your business? Does it provide you all the necessary data to make decisions?
- How will a buyer perceive your company by reviewing these reports and systems?

Notes:

Backbone of Business: Key Systems for Support Functions

When a buyer comes into the picture, they will ask you all kinds of questions. Sometimes, it might be information you haven't even thought about. In general, it's good practice to have these systems in place, but it's becoming increasingly important to show separation between the business and you, the owner. Remember, the new management team should be able to take over seamlessly, and that includes managing all internal operations and support functions.

Streamline payroll, HR, onboarding, offboarding, and benefits administration through systems. Using tools like Zenefits, Gusto or BambooHR can enhance operational efficiency, reduce manual errors, and ensure compliance with regulatory requirements. QuickBooks or Xero can automate accounting processes, monthly invoicing, following up on delayed payments, etc. Tools such as Ramp or Brex will enforce processes for reimbursements, travel bookings, and payments. Automating lead generation and campaign management can help nurture leads and bring them into the system.

> Pro tip. Your EBITDA dictates your valuation, as we will discuss in detail during the next section. At ITTDigital, I didn't have an HR manager or a finance manager to help run the business. Instead, I used systems and processes and a wonderful executive assistant, who was based in LATAM, and we were doing over $10 million in revenue. Any other help was outsourced and fractional to keep costs extremely low and the core team efficient.

Each of these systems is an asset to the business that clearly creates value through saving time and money. Each system is followed by a process, and each process should become an SOP added to the Operations Handbook. This process manual will eliminate decision fatigue across the organization and allow team members to propel the organization forward. It also provides the buyer with a reference manual so your attention can be elsewhere during the transition period.

The Operations Handbook: The Blueprint for Success

An Operations Handbook is a living document that includes detailed process maps, standard operating procedures (SOPs), and guidelines for every critical function within the business. This handbook is essential for ensuring consistency and continuity, especially when transitioning to new ownership. It outlines how each department operates, how tasks are performed, and who is responsible for what, ensuring that the business can run smoothly even in the absence of its key players.

For small business owners looking to sell their company, an Operations Handbook is invaluable. It provides a clear, documented reference for every process within the business, ensuring that the incoming buyer can seamlessly take over. This handbook proves that your organization is well-organized, documented, and capable of running smoothly even in your absence.

Creating an Operations Handbook may seem daunting, but it can be done efficiently with the right approach. Delegate this task to your EA or another capable team member. They can interview team members, create process maps, and develop step-by-step guides. Using tools like ChatGPT can

further streamline the creation of process documents, ensuring consistency and thoroughness. Once the initial draft is ready, have the team review it to ensure accuracy and completeness.

When a potential buyer evaluates your business, they are looking for assurance that the company can continue to thrive without its current owner. A detailed Operations Handbook offers this assurance by demonstrating that every process is documented, from sales and project management to HR and payroll. This transparency reduces perceived risk, making your business more attractive and valuable.

To ensure that your Operations Handbook remains relevant and effective, it should be audited and updated quarterly. This process doesn't have to be time-consuming. With tools like Chat-GPT, your executive assistant can quickly identify and implement process improvements. Regular updates will keep the handbook current, showcase continuous improvement to the organization, and impress potential buyers. In many cases, processes don't change, and we just need to update a few dates and confirm that the document was reviewed.

An updated Operations Handbook also helps identify manual and time-consuming processes that can be automated. This is a crucial step in enhancing operational efficiency and scalability. Automating repetitive tasks frees up valuable time for your team to focus on higher-value activities. We'll discuss more on Cognitive Automation in a later section of the book.

Even if you choose not to exit, this is a valuable tool to create autonomy within the organization, and reduce your workload.

FORCE Exercise: Reflect on your Operations Handbook.

- Does your team always come to you to solve their problems? Is there a way to reduce the time you spend supporting others?

- Do you know the processes your teams are following? When was the handbook last updated?

- Have you evaluated any processes that are extremely time-consuming for automation?

Notes:

Data Management: Transforming Insights into Action

Once you have the Operations Handbook in place, you should identify how to drive the company with data and use data for future decision-making. Your buyer is going to ask for data; some could be related to sales, others to delivery, and others could be related to HR, payroll, and finances, etc. The key here is to create an automated dashboard for each key member of your team. This dashboard should provide all the data they require to do their job effectively and make decisions. There are many examples of great dashboards online, and you should ensure each dashboard is catered to your business.

In order to do this, you need to understand the data that each role may require. As the CEO of the company, what information do you request from your associates? This is the high-level requirement for each dashboard that should flow up to yours. Your key team members may want additional information to be included in their individual dashboards, which is perfectly fine; let's ensure they have it! To create these dashboards, we can leverage tools such as Google Data Studio, renamed Looker Studio, which is free. There are, of course, other tools that can be used, so explore those options and see what works best for you.

Using Looker Studio, you can take data from almost any CRM system, PM system, financial system, or HR system and integrate it in real time to generate visual reports. Again, you should not waste time doing this manually; you should set it up once and have someone on the team make minor updates and corrections or work with a cost effective contractor that can make updates as needed. This may feel like an arduous task, but once it's put in place, you will have all data points at your fingertips.

I love data, and I decided to hire someone internally for both my companies, but we don't want to increase our expenses when we are about to position a sale. Could you imagine how much you save when you have an update meeting and no one needs to prepare a PowerPoint presentation or put the data together? In my case, my EA has always had to chase my sales leaders and delivery leaders to get the data together because they are always so busy with client deliverables and escalations that they feel this is a waste of time. I get it—we all have our priority tasks, and internal action items like these rarely make the cut. But as the business owners, it's important for us to have this data and ensure our teams are doing their job effectively. They are faced with daily pressures from clients, and we need to respect that. So it's up to us to find a way to meet them in the middle, and dashboards are a great approach to that.

Could you imagine how this looks to a potential acquirer? As they review your company, you can share these dashboards with them, stressing that the data is real-time and verified by the team to ensure accuracy and support quick decision-making. Leveraging data analytics to make informed strategic decisions, monitor performance, and identify trends can significantly enhance your business's efficiency and attractiveness to potential buyers. This approach helps improve performance, reduce costs, and demonstrates that your business is well-managed and sustainable.

On a side note, as part of Operational Excellence, it's important to backup all internal data and client data, especially if the client deliverables are digital. At ITTDigital, I've had clients come back after three years requesting data files of old projects for enhancements and upgrades, and if we weren't able to provide them with what they needed, we may have lost their trust entirely. It also might be a part of your contract to retain this information in case there is a loss at the client's end. It's important to have an infrastructure process in place to manage software subscriptions and other assets in the business. We will go deeper into this in the Resource Maximization section.

FORCE Exercise: Reflect on data management within your organization.

- How do team members use data in your organization today?
- Does your team spend a lot of time internally creating presentations for management requests? Can that time be put toward something else?
- What are the data sources your team is using? Do you know if they're accurate enough to make important decisions?

Notes:

Elevating Customer Experience: Beyond Satisfaction

Last, it all comes down to this—the final big operational topic, Customer Experience. You want customers to be delighted with everything you do and want them to come back with their pockets open for more! Each aspect of Operational Excellence eventually flows into creating a better experience for our customers, stakeholders, employees, and ourselves as business owners which ultimately helps sell our business!

Systems and processes combined with autonomous decision-making and data at your fingertips make it much easier to focus on the important aspects of growth. It helps reduce the clutter on your calendar and the constant follow-up for information from busy parties. When all this is done properly, you can sit back and watch the business take care of itself and remove yourself from the day-to-day activities which will help you ultimately exit the business, Maximizing Founder Value under the most favorable terms.

Improving customer service starts with gauging where you stand today. Your team can create a simple Jotform or Google Form survey for free and get quick feedback from customers. I usually incorporated this as part of the closing or feedback loop within projects, whether the engagement went well or not. While some projects might have fallen short of customer expectations, we can still gauge our ability to communicate effectively, send reports, problem solve, and determine long-term client satisfaction. It's important to keep these reports short and simple and there are a ton of examples online that can easily be adopted. We don't need to use any complicated tools or systems, just request general feedback via email and keep it for our records. We can go as far as to link bonuses or other incentives for internal team members to these surveys so clients take them to ensure team members are compensated for their efforts.

Once we have some data, commit to resolve issues efficiently, enhance customer satisfaction, and ensure that your business is running smoothly and efficiently. By improving your customer service, you can make your business more attractive to potential buyers. Imagine how this looks when you can show a report like this to your buyers with a trend line showing customer experience improving over a period of time. This shows your ability to generate business in the long run and that you truly understand your customers. Buyers want this; it reduces risk, creates a compelling argument to their higher-ups, and makes you ever so desirable.

Let's Exit By FORCE!

FORCE Exercise: Reflect on your operational house.

- How do you feel about Operational Excellence within your business?
- Can you prove to a buyer that business can run without you and is completely de-risked?
- What is your game plan to execute on the strategy and steps listed above?
- **Weapons: Review the Operational Excellence Checklist in the Exit By FORCE Toolkit located at ExitByFORCE.com/Weapons**

Notes:

STEP 3: RESOURCE MAXIMIZATION

Imagine managing a house where resources are poorly allocated—some rooms are freezing while other areas of the house are leaking. If you're not careful, studies show you're capable of spending an extra $25,000/year on wasted utilities. Imagine what you could do if you found $25,000 in your pocket one day? That's the impact of effective resource management. The same principles apply to managing a business.

Attractive businesses excel at doing more with less, maximizing output, minimizing waste, and improving profitability. It creates a compelling story that appeals to buyers. This section focuses on ensuring that your allocated dollars are paying off and providing the desired results. Managing numbers is essential to show that your business is moving in the right direction. One key metric is revenue per headcount.

The Revenue Per Headcount Approach[33,34,35]

Running a business involves managing countless data points. The challenge lies in collecting the right data and ensuring its accuracy to make informed decisions. Too much data can create decision fatigue, which I'm sure you've experienced and found frustrating. One major metric that is a good indicator of resource efficiency is revenue per headcount. The metric is self-explanatory, and how to calculate headcount is given below. Ideally, as revenue increases, this metric will trend in a positive direction, showing a well-run business. If your costs go up faster than revenue, there is a potential problem.

In general, our job as business owners is to generate profits and reward our shareholders; the same goes for potential buyers. Revenue per headcount gives us an easy way to calculate the measure of costs associated with generating revenue, and is widely looked at by buyers. This gives buyers a good indication of the business's ability to scale and if there are adequate profits to reinvest in the business. Headcount is used because it is generally our most expensive resource for small businesses, so this metric is a good indicator of how well we are managing our resources. If our revenue per headcount is increasing, it indicates that our team is becoming more efficient and productive.

Many years ago at Apple, before Steve Jobs returned, the management team was working on producing twenty different laptop devices at the same time. The company was bleeding cash at the time, and was doing too much. Each laptop project had its own use case, customer market, and complexity, requiring specialized teams of engineers, marketers, supply chain managers, and more. This, of course, dropped the revenue per headcount trend for Apple. When Steve Jobs returned, he threw sixteen prototypes out the window, telling the management team he would focus on developing four and ONLY four different products at one time. He explained to the management team that ultimately having twenty different devices was illogical and unscalable. It required too much investment, and would also confuse buyers.[36] He consolidated teams, skyrocketing revenue per headcount, reinvested the cash to generate new products, and this gave us the iMac, iPod, iPad, and the iPhone. Steve Jobs knew the importance of revenue per headcount; it helps us understand our ability to scale and reinvest in the future. This is an important measurement, so let's ensure we have it available for acquirers.

We might be tempted to cheat on the headcount part of the business. For instance, instead of hiring an internal team member, we could hire a contractor, which would decrease headcount and create a positive trend. Here's how you should think about it—your headcount should include both direct and indirect team members working on the business. You can exclude anyone contributing less than twenty hours per week and anyone in training such as interns. Legal services, accountants, project-based vendors, or those paid on a purely variable basis should be excluded. If someone is doing at least twenty hours per week, count them as half a person. For example, if you outsource your recruitment team and pay an hourly rate for a dedicated resource, this will count toward your headcount. On the other hand, if you pay a placement fee for a successful hire to the recruiter or to the recruitment company, this will be excluded from the denominator.

Now that we understand the definition of the metric, let's plot a trend line over the last year and see how we can make strategic decisions to influence the trend in an upward direction. You are where you are today, so take stock with a goal of improvement moving forward. We will focus on high-value areas and take our time to avoid disrupting the business. Implementing the changes below that influence this metric can affect internal stakeholders, client experiences, and the overall well-being of the company, so we must make the right decisions.

When done properly, this will significantly enhance your valuation and ability to attract buyers. Buyers will see the scalability of your business; it will help validate your EBITDA and will get you a higher multiplier during negotiations. As we are looking to exit, feel free to incorporate a bit of salesmanship.

FORCE Exercise: Reflect on the revenue per headcount metric.

- Do you feel this could be a good indicator for your business? Is this something you have measured before?
- What actions could you take to influence this number?
- Are there any other expenses on par with labor that could be a good indicator for you?

Notes:

Workforce Efficiency and the Family Factor

No one wants to talk about workforce efficiency; it's the toughest and the worst part of the job. As small business owners those who were there from the beginning often feel like family. As we scale and grow, we may realize these team members no longer fit in the ecosystem the way they once did, perhaps due to the changes in skills required as the company grows. Yet, we keep them in the organization, dreading to part ways. This happens too often and sometimes it helps the company, but more often than not, it hurts the company.

We understand that these are people with families relying on them or new college graduates just getting their feet wet. They are people with hopes and dreams who rely on your business. The truth is, if you don't take an outside-in look at the workforce, someone else will, and they will make these decisions without remorse which could be worse for your team.

> If you haven't recently, take a critical look at your workforce and think about the contributions of all top-level employees, especially those that have risen through the ranks over years (maybe even decades). Ask yourself what their strengths and weaknesses are, and whether they fit into the company you are now looking to sell. Do they add significant cost burdens? Are they really well equipped to do their job under a change of ownership? Are you perhaps doing them a disservice by keeping them in employment in a place no longer suited for them?

These decisions are tough, but remember, your acquirer will likely make these changes regardless. It's better for you to make the tough decisions and gain the value from them. If your business is harboring family members or other close relations that are sensitive, there's no need for you to act—the buyer will handle it in the future, and they can be the bad guy. Just understand the value you may be leaving on the table. As long as the opportunity cost makes sense to you, only do what you are comfortable with. I would consider this an area of high stakes as it's your reputation and your relationships. I would rather be in control of this situation, even if people are not thrilled with me in the short term, and ensure people can transition easily with adequate time. When the stakes are high, always be in control.

One of the businesses that entered the Exit By FORCE accelerator program was an eighty-person marketing agency with over $18 Million in revenue operated with twelve close knit family members that all held C-level and director-level positions in the organization. When I say close, I mean CLOSE. All twelve family members were children, siblings, cousins, and family friends. The organization was looking to exit, and within four months had two potential buyers that had asked to see their financials. The team knew they were minutes away from taking a closer look at the org chart and understanding that this was a family-run business. Luckily, the owner's family truly excelled at business. Seven of those twelve were meant for the jobs and titles they held; unfortunately, the other five were no longer positively contributing. The owner had a decision to make here.

Despite our protests, he decided to keep all twelve family members in the business when he sold, and understandably so—this allowed him to "do right by his family," which was more important to him than getting the best possible deal from the sale. We supported him; this is not an uncommon decision. The business sold for 11X on EBITDA, an excellent price, especially after the accelerator unlocked an additional $700,000 in EBITDA.

However, within a year, the buyers let go of every single family member, citing concerns over information leaking. If our client had heeded our suggestions, at least with the five non-contributing family members, he would have unlocked an additional $600,000 in EBITDA, adding at 11X an additional $6.6 Million in valuation, giving him the ability to pay each family member, including the others let go later, close to half a million dollars as severance.

In this case it's all hindsight bias—he wished he'd followed our plan of action and done exactly that. I do believe he made the right decision for himself, regardless of what he may think of that decision at this point. It was an extremely tough situation that he was in. This case study illustrates a small business that had all the best intentions and ended up regretting the decision to keep all the family members. He later realized that buyers will make these decisions anyway and it would have been better if he had control over communicating with family members and ensuring they had a peaceful transition.

FORCE Exercise: Reflect on personal relationships within your organization.

- Are you keeping team members based on a relationship?
- Do you have other relationships to consider such as vendors and partners where you may be able to get a more cost-effective service?
- How much value are you willing to give up to be the good guy or gal?

Notes:

Business Outflows: Where Your Money Goes

Once you've dealt with the hardest stuff, close relationships, let's take a look at your delivery wing. If your business is an hourly business, meaning you don't need a lot of full-time internal team members and you pay mostly on an hourly basis, such as purely time and material, feel free to skip this section. Your business is probably running as lean as possible.

If you employ most of your team full-time, such as recruiters, software engineers, account managers, and supporting roles, it's vital to manage your largest cost center closely. At both of my companies, I had most of my delivery team hired full time and it was essential that I watched the numbers here closely. A single extra hire and profitability will drop significantly. To manage this, recall the Operational Excellence section, where we spoke about a project management tool that measures utilization rate or productivity of the team. This is where your hard work pays off.

The utilization report will tell you if any of your team members are overworked or sitting idle on the bench. You will never get this perfect, but it's important to get as close as possible to managing the full-time workforce to 90% utilization or higher. Where does your utilization rate stand today? If you are under the 90% mark, you have a few more workforce efficiencies to figure out. I understand you may win new work at any time and I've addressed how to tackle this with partners to ensure you have a flexible workforce in place below. You are looking to exit, so it's imperative to manage your workforce as lean as possible, to maximize EBITDA and your multiplier.

In today's virtual world, it's easy to find cost-effective and great talent on freelance platforms such as Upwork or Fiverr. Since we are discussing this through the lens of an exit, you need to see if there are other avenues to maximize EBITDA. Thus, consider if you have team members that can become fractional, outsourced, or offshored. Especially, take a look at support functions that don't show up on the utilization report. Are all of your internal HR and support team members fully occupied?

When we are honest with ourselves, we may find that many of our team members are wasting valuable time on unnecessary activities. These decisions are tough, and that's when an external agency, such as Kenobi Capital, can help evaluate without bias and be the bad guy, so you, as the business owner, are always looked at in a good light. Of course, we need to ensure that there is no deterioration in operations throughout this process.

One hire I would recommend is an executive assistant. This role will save you countless hours managing non-value-added activities so you can focus on what's important: your exit. If you already have this role with another title such as admin or chief of staff, fantastic. If not, it's important to hire an executive assistant to help drive all the initiatives in this book and be the front-facing follow-up person to save you countless hours. You can find top-tier talent on freelance portals listed above; there are also many agencies providing executive assistant if you prefer to go that route. If someone in your company can take on this role, that's even better; let's assign them to it. Just keep in mind the skill set is important.

At ITTDigital, we were growing rapidly, and the finance team grew with it before we had systems and processes in place that matched scale. Once those systems were implemented, most of the work was automated, and the team created busy work to justify their existence, and this led to massive unnecessary expenses for the business. We recognized the issue for what it was and ended up outsourcing the entire team to a friend's firm, and the efficiency and professionalism increased significantly at one-third the cost.

Just to make sure we are on the same page, none of the above means that full-time team members are unnecessary. Full-time team members, in most cases, are truly dedicated and work much harder than external resources, and I've always preferred to hire team members full time for core business services that must be under our control. The team makes up the company and controls the entire experience; it's vital to have a great team. At the same time, we need to consider our profitability at exit.

One way to still hire full-time staff is to find the right ratio of onshore to offshore team members. I understand that many business owners may not have exposure or may have had a poor experience managing offshore teams, but when done properly, it adds significant value. Both of my companies had teams offshore in a full-time capacity to support the USA-based team members. This not only makes onshore team members' productivity jump significantly and impress our customers, it also drives profits and reinvesting savings to grow. These team members are fully dedicated at 25% of the cost of their onshore counterparts.

We must ensure our core business goes unaffected while making these changes and manage this process carefully. I've found tremendous success working with people from India, LATAM, low-cost EU areas, and the Philippines. There is great talent around the world, and it's ours for the taking. Saving a few hundred thousand dollars will increase your valuation by millions at exit.

FORCE Exercise: Reflect on your business's utilization rate.

- Have you calculated your utilization rate and used it for decision-making?
- Can any of the positions in your company become fractional, outsourced, or offshored?
- How large is your internal support team versus the rest of your internal team?

Notes:

Dynamic Teams: The Flex Advantage

We never want to lose business or not take on work due to bandwidth issues, and we also want to manage a high utilization of personnel, somewhere around 90%. Considering this, we need a plan in place in case we receive additional, unexpected client work. It's surprising how many times I've heard small businesses say they don't have the capacity for more. Building capacity and scale is essential to your business. Imagine not taking up a project that could have cascaded into millions of dollars' worth of additional work, or not taking a Fortune 500 client. Why let go of that opportunity? This is where a flex team comes into the picture. A flex team is like an extension of your own team, but employed by partners. The best way to set up a flex team is to find three to four fantastic partners you can lean on as needed.

Partners are small businesses similar to yours that would be happy to work in the background. They have a similar skill set, can deliver to the quality you expect, and are trustworthy and reliable. Finding new partners can be challenging because, in most cases, they are untested, add a level of risk and complexity, and let's be honest, we don't have complete control over them. Yet, they are vital to increasing capacity and managing costs. At ITTDigital, we always had an explosion of work toward the end of the year as corporate budgets were expiring. We set up four partners, smaller technology firms, to help us with the additional work, and the client had no idea partners were in the background.

To test each partner, put them on inactive delivered projects simulated as an active project. We never let our partners interface directly with the client, so our project managers and project teams would simulate client requests, and the partner had to deliver to the timeline. We went through twelve partners to finalize four partners that we called the Fantastic Four. The effort was worth it because it gave us the ability to scale quickly and keep our overheads extremely low. The best part: we never had to let go of team members for lack of work, and only hired when we could guarantee long-term work. Again, aim for 90% utilization in your own team. It's surprising that, sometimes, partners can be more efficient and cost-effective than we are, and this exposure allows us to integrate the partner's practices into our own business.

Once we had the Fantastic Four in place, with contracts negotiated and working processes set, addressing new capacity was never an issue. We were able to win new business and drive larger profits. This increased EBITDA, lowered risk, and led to higher valuations!

Vendor Management: Where Subscriptions Go to Die

A key aspect of managing resources is a vendor management team. Vendor management team is a loose description; this could be one person such as a COO or CFO who has overall responsibility, or an executive assistant reviewing all expenses and subscriptions monthly and questioning team members. From Google Workspace or Microsoft Office to our internet and phone provider to accounting software, CRM, a project management tool, Slack, or Zoom, anything we spend on externally is a vendor. My EA was responsible for auditing all licenses on a month basis; we didn't have a single software license that was not utilized, regardless of cost. Any expense takes away from the available resources of the business and the opportunity cost of investing those dollars somewhere else. Thus, we have to manage it closely and maintain control!

> When was the last time you reviewed the number of email accounts you had open in the organization? Is there a review and audit process in place? This is where your executive assistant gets handy. Create a document of all the external expenses in the organization. This should be easy with a quick review of the monthly credit card statements or QuickBooks. Ensure you have all the usernames and passwords centrally controlled so your EA can log in to any admin account. If accounts are individual, set up a company account for that vendor. Once you have this, go and negotiate relentlessly with them. You will see a drastic drop in your expenses!

Feel free to replace vendors as well; your EA can do the research and find the best tool for the company as a better price point. You have to audit each licensed subscription at least quarterly and ensure the business is not losing money to wasted subscriptions. Think about how many subscriptions we waste on the personal side; a business is way worse! You would be surprised how many business owners have never deleted an email address from their system. If you don't tell someone to do it, it will never be done. $10 per month per employee with many people joining and leaving over the last few years is thousands of dollars a year and hundreds of thousands in lost valuation.

Don't take this lightly! Be in control when the stakes are high and the stakes are always high where money is involved.

I was directly involved in resource management. Some areas are easy, such as subscription licenses and software tools, which can be left to other team members. More complicated negotiations, where stakes were high, were handled directly by me. Only I understood the value of the savings at hand and knew how it would affect my business valuation at the time of exit. Read *Never Split the Difference* by Chris Voss to give you tips on how to win negotiations. It worked fantastically for me. Get involved in this process.[37]

Last, keep risk management always on your mind. While it's great to take these actions and save dollar bills, you don't want the business going under because of it. It's important to take your time and ensure the changes you make don't destroy something. Expert advice could save you time and money, especially in areas of offshoring and vendor negotiations. Ensure you develop comprehensive strategies to mitigate risks within the supply chain, including diversifying your suppliers, building trust, and having a plan B for everything!

By focusing on these key areas, you can significantly enhance your business's profitability and valuation, positioning it as a desirable acquisition target, and keeping everything within your control. Remember, attractive businesses excel at doing more with less, creating a compelling narrative for potential buyers.

Let's Exit By FORCE!

FORCE Exercise: Reflect on your house's resources.

- How do you feel about Resource Maximization within your business?
- Have you taken all the steps that you are comfortable with to maximize your EBITDA?
- What is your game plan to execute the strategy and steps listed above?
- **Weapons: Review the Resource Maximization Checklist in the Exit By FORCE Toolkit located at ExitByFORCE.com/Weapons**

Notes:

STEP 4: COGNITIVE AUTOMATION

Are we home yet? Imagine driving up to your house and the lights turn on as you enter, the thermostat adjusts to your preferred temperature, and a robot vacuum is quietly cleaning the floors. Your car auto parks itself in the garage and gets plugged into the charger; it's like magic! Your business should operate with the same level of seamless automation. Incorporating Cognitive Automation is the combination of AI and Robotic Process Automation (RPA) that mimics human intelligence and behavior.

Incorporating this into your operations not only sets you apart but also positions your business as an innovative and tech play for growth and scale. It also demonstrates that the business can run smoothly without your day-to-day intervention, proving that the management team can easily take over. Cognitive Automation isn't just about technology; it's about creating significant value, driving innovation, and saving time.

Harnessing Automation: Real-World Examples from the Giants

Consider Tesla, a company that has embraced automation at every level. From its manufacturing processes to its customer interactions, Tesla uses automation to drive efficiency and innovation. For instance, Tesla's Gigafactories are highly automated, with robots handling a significant portion of the manufacturing process. This not only speeds up production but also ensures high quality and consistency. Tesla's approach to automation has allowed it to scale rapidly and maintain a competitive edge in the automotive industry.[38]

Similarly, Amazon has revolutionized logistics and supply chain management through automation. Amazon's fulfillment centers are equipped with advanced robotics and AI systems that manage inventory, pick and pack orders, and optimize delivery routes. This level of automation enables Amazon to process millions of orders efficiently and deliver them to customers quickly. The company's commitment to automation has been a key factor in its ability to scale and dominate the e-commerce market.[39,40,41]

Of course, these are big players with unlimited budgets. Let's see how we can implement similar practices within our small business to enhance profits, simplify our lives, and for freedom!

Reinventing Efficiency: Process Optimization Strategies[42,43,44]

Automation starts with reviewing our processes. In the Operational Excellence chapter, we established the importance of an Operations Handbook and process mapping across the business. In the Resource Maximization chapter, we looked into resource spending, whether it's people, software tools, or partners, and how the handbook and resourcing go hand in hand. We understand the back-end flow of our business like the back of our hand. For automation, we need to ensure we are doing everything as efficiently as possible. Are there steps in our processes that can be removed or are unnecessary? Could there be something burdening the organization that might not be warranted? Let's see how process optimization can make the business more efficient, driving utilization and efficiency, or, as I call it, magic!

Utilize process mapping to understand operational workflows, and identify areas of bottlenecks, redundancies, and inefficiencies for targeted improvements. Process mapping involves creating a visual representation of your business processes; it helps you understand how things are currently done and identify areas for improvement. This is not only a great additional for your Operations Handbook, but, by mapping out your processes, you can use the visual representation to identify areas for improvement. Visual processes are always easier to understand. There are many tools available online that can help you with the visualization.

Once you have process maps to complement the Operations Handbook, let's seek out inefficiencies within current operations where you can implement process or technological improvements, thereby reducing waste and lowering operational costs. In many instances, processes were set when the company first started operations and haven't been updated since. With advances in technology and automation, you should revisit these processes and determine if there is a better way to go about it.

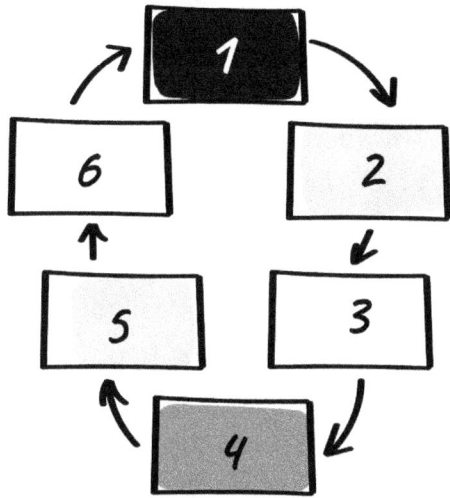

Try something as simple as SEO. There are now tools that will automate 100% of this process so that we can eliminate any internal actions, and they're much more cost-effective. I really like the SEO tool called Seona, its new on the market as of 2024. See if you can do this for other areas of your business. We should look at the business with a fine-tooth comb to identify areas for improvement, and then figure out if there is a solution that works. Of course, it helps to already know the solutions in the market, and sometimes that's when an expert can add a lot of value and save time.

You may now have an idea where automation can be implemented within your company.

Remember, the business process comes first, and you are using technology to solve a specific problem.

Do not look at this from a technology first angle. You need to understand the problem you are solving and be able to numerically track that our actions made an impact. Once areas are identified, invest in technology that does the process better, faster, and smarter. Make sure it saves you time and elevates everyone's experience. We spoke about where you should make key investments for long-term business growth in previous sections; this is one of those areas. By investing in the right solutions, you can ensure that your business runs smoothly and efficiently, making it a technology company and more attractive to potential buyers.

This is a high stakes area in your business; doing this properly can add significant value that you didn't even know existed. You don't know what you don't know, but this is an area to take control and drive. When the stakes are high, always be in control!

I suggest we tackle low-hanging fruit before we move into more complex automation strategies. These items can easily be done on your own or by your team, but take caution when implementing automation in high-impact areas that could have cascading effects across the business.

FORCE Exercise: Reflect on process optimization.

- When was the last time you reviewed the processes in your organization? Can something be done better?
- Do you see any bottlenecks in your process? Can technology be applied to help?
- What is your exposure to automation? Do you have someone in your network that can guide you?

Notes:

Attack of the Clones: The Low-Hanging Fruit

HR on Autopilot: Streamlining Employee Management: Implement end-to-end automation for HR processes using a platform like Zenefits. This automation covers onboarding, offboarding, managing benefits, 401(k) plans, and pay slips with minimal manual intervention. Ensure any service you select also files all payroll taxes and takes care of compliance with different states, especially in our remote working era. Designate an assistant to oversee and manage these processes to ensure smooth and efficient operations. If the business pays team members on an hourly basis, ensure the tool you select has a good time sheet addition or integrates well and has an approval mechanism. OpenProject does a good job for the hourly billing aspect.

The goal here is self-service: team members onboard themselves, enter their data and verification requirements, sign everything digitally (stored in records), and manage their benefits and insurance claims independently. Your executive assistant can get involved for smaller items and to trigger onboarding and off-boarding documents, reducing manual labor requirements. You may already have someone handling this work. If it's you, all the more reason to implement a tool and reduce your time on this low-value add activity. If it's someone else, make them automate it! As I said before, ITTDigital was doing $10+ million in revenue and my executive assistant was my HR representative. Anything that she couldn't handle with the tool, which was uncommon, was outsourced.

Financial Automation: Letting Numbers Work for You: Using automation tools within QuickBooks or Xero will remove almost all manual intervention when managing finances. These tools have become extremely advanced and, once set up, take care of everything! Of course, we are talking about money and need to be in full control. It's best not to remove the human element completely—but we want to ensure any manual labor, which translates into costs, is minimized.

Your current accounting team should be able to put these automations in place. This should include recurring invoices, accounts receivable follow-ups, late fee assessments, employee reimbursements, payment approvals and scheduling, and weekly closings. This ensures financial data is accurate and readily available for decision-making, streamlining your financial operations and providing you with up-to-date financial insights. You probably have a team in place, so ensure they work on this as a project and get it done.

Support System Overhaul: Automating Back-end Operations: The same process you used for HR and Finance can be applied to all other support functions in the organization. Let's look at the IT team. Do you get requests to create email addresses or allocate licenses for specific tools? This entire process can be automated using a customer support ticketing tool where everything is tracked and reported. Once this is set up, you'll be able to see dashboards on open tasks and tickets, ensuring everything gets done in a timely manner. This applies to client support activities as well as internal tools such as Adobe, cloud services, phone lines, and equipment. Think about other support functions in your organization that can be automated. Let's make it a priority and automate it, especially if there are costs associated with it. Of course, each business is different, so make sure you have the right personnel to address something super technical or that requires specific knowledge.

The Bottom Line: Real-time Data Dashboards: When working with systems and processes, set them up to auto-generate real-time data and dashboards across the organization. Ensure all team members can access relevant and current data snapshots as required, fostering a data-driven culture and informed decision-making. This helps you make more informed decisions without creating presentations or coordinating between teams. An added bonus is implementing a tool like ChatGPT to query the data. This is more advanced and can be added to the end of the process. For now, get the dashboards up and running without manual intervention.

Digital Dynamo: Automating Presence and Lead Gen: Deploy AI tools across your marketing and lead generation teams such as Seona, Dall-E or MailerLite. These tools can enhance SEO, design, content creation, and campaign management. By leveraging AI, you can optimize your marketing efforts, generate more leads, and improve your overall marketing strategy. This strategy should include end-to-end social media automation (LinkedIn, Facebook, Instagram, YouTube, X (Twitter), or any other platforms you use).

In my firm, I've used Airtable to organize ninety posts so I can post three times a day on each platform on autopilot; it's magic! I review the posts once a month for a few minutes, have my EA make any relevant changes, and done. Reach out if you need best practices on doing this; it's quick and easy with a few shortcuts. There are many tools that can be used for lead generation as well.

For email marketing, consider MailChimp or MailerLite. MailerLite may be cheaper for smaller businesses; I started out with it. The same goes for LinkedIn lead generation, ad campaigns, and addressing any inbound leads from your website or other sources. Last, simple automations like using a calendar booking tool like Calendly and an email grammar and editing tool like Grammarly can significantly streamline your operations. Implement each of these as assets to your business and review them monthly or quarterly based on visibility and priority.

These are just a few of the low-hanging fruit to consider which can be addressed easily. In fact, many of these tools are made for small businesses, but most small business owners are not great at taking advantage of them. Especially owners that are not exposed to these advancements or are tech averse. I hope your business has already incorporated automation to this extent, but if not, there is no better time than now. It's imperative to get it done for the exit process and claim that we use automation across the organization to get those tech valuations!

When you're set up like this, it counts as automation. Make sure you claim it. You are using AI tools to reduce manual labor. It doesn't have to be something extremely complex like Machine Learning (ML) or Robotic Process Automation (RPA) to be considered automation. Buyers will love this; you are now considered a tech play for investment purposes. This will help drive valuations once positioned properly.

It's time to visit some of the more complex topics. This can be implemented on your own; however, if you are not exposed or an expert in these areas, I suggest finding an expert to help you or guide you along the way. More complicated automations create significant value, but if done incorrectly, they can hurt your business, and we don't want that during your exit process.

FORCE Exercise: Reflect on basic automation within your business.

- What is your automation philosophy? Do you encourage team members to be innovative?
- Are there other key areas of your business that can be addressed?
- Do you have capable leaders you can delegate to who can implement automation within their respective areas?

Notes:

Next-level Automation: Case Studies and Examples

In order to explain these high-end strategies, I'm going to showcase two real examples that worked wonderfully within my businesses. As each business is different and has different processes, you will have to think about which are your high-value areas that can be automated using this thought process.

Example 1: IT Trailblazers LLC is a staffing firm focused on contract and temporary staffing. We had many clients who would release requirements on vendor management systems (VMS) such as SAP Fieldglass, a cloud-based vendor management software. Each system had similar processes for us to submit candidates into the system, which took a recruiter an additional forty-five minutes of administrative time. We considered this forty-five minutes an annoying cost of doing business a.k.a. a waste of time because we didn't know if our candidate would get selected, and if another company submitted the same candidate before us, they got priority. So, we used a tool called Selenium, an open-source web-based automation tool, to speed this process up.

We started by understanding each VMS and the various client processes that we had to follow. We then created a process map for the four largest tools based on the most complicated client procedures we had to follow. We used the most complicated process because we could use it across clients that had easier processes without any rework. Once ready, we created a repository of all the fields needed to submit a candidate in the portal, which was autofilled by our applicant tracking system. Finally, we launched the tool.

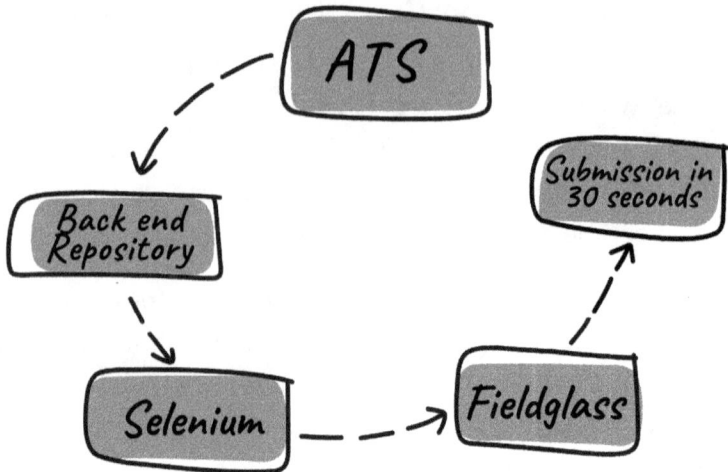

The results were outstanding. The process that took forty-five minutes per candidate submission was reduced to thirty seconds per submission. Each recruiter saved over two hours per day, and the organization saved over 200 hours per day. At a cost of $40 per hour, that's $8,000 per day, $180,000 per month, or $2.2 million per year. Additionally, we were able to increase recruiter submission counts from three to five per day, boosting company revenue by 30% without any additional expense. Of course, the tool needed occasional updates to avoid operational slowdowns, but we could easily allocate a small budget for this and continue building on the automation. This just goes to show exactly how powerful automation can be when used appropriately. IT Trailblazers' top line quadrupled in four years as we implemented data and automation strategies.

Example 2: Here is another example for you from ITTDigital, a web development agency using advanced open-source technologies such as Drupal. Each project we worked on required a variety of skill sets for proper execution, meaning we used to staff front-end developers, back-end developers, quality assurance engineers, project managers, business analysis, etc. The first 30% of each project followed a similar flow: spinning up development environments, creating instances and infrastructure, and setting the foundation. The remaining 70% was highly customized for each client, and subsequently, each project.

We wrote a process map for the first 30% of each project, using the most complex requirements. This ensured it was all-encompassing and even if the client didn't require it, they appreciated it as a free add on bonus. We then created a small automation application within the Drupal framework with our existing team members. When new projects came in, with a click of a button we were able to complete the first 30% of any project, saving countless hours of effort. It was magic, like real Hogwarts magic! This reduced project timelines, allowed the same team to handle more projects, reduced reliance on vendors, and increased profits. We could keep the same pricing structure, give the client an expedited timeline, and keep the profits for ourselves! When faced with competitive pricing, we could lower our prices and win new business without sacrificing margins. That's Gryffindor status!

Trust in the FORCE. This can be done for your organization as well. Whether you run a senior healthcare facility or a construction business, there is always room for advanced automation if you know where to look. Reach out and consult one of our FORCE experts if you're curious about what kinds of efficiencies might bring you the biggest ROIs.

Any business that uses templates or submits proposals like RFPs and RFQs can be automated, and tools like Chat-GPT can add a layer of advanced automation for end-to-end proposals. Any business requiring cost estimation can use advanced automation techniques to automate the process, even for complex government projects with bonding requirements. I'm sure, if you look closely enough, you will find manual processes that do not require a human touch where you can save countless hours and measure return on investment.

While I don't recommend implementing on your own, especially if you lack the expertise, it's worth exploring how this can impact your business. Take small steps to see if you can identify areas where this will help and give you an ROI. My suggestion is to start with the low-hanging fruit and observe the impact on your time and money. Once proof of concept is established, you can consider more advanced techniques that can drive your business to new heights.

Automation is a significant game-changer, and new tools arrive on the market every day. It's important to keep up with the latest technology, which often comes at a cheaper price point. We should also consider the cost of switching tools and implementing a new process before we start down that path. I don't recommend "experimentation" here—if you don't know what you're doing, find someone who does. I know many a business owner who lost their shirt on a bad deal, and were stuck in some sort of major commitment with tools that simply did not fit their businesses. Last, the order is important; don't skip to Cognitive

Automation without completing the other three sections (Financial Optimization, Operational Excellence, and Resource Maximization). Otherwise, there is a good chance that you will have to do it all over again.

Great work so far! Keep reading the book—you're almost ready to sell your business. It doesn't matter what industry you're in; you're now a high-tech business and will command tech valuations.

If anyone asks what you do, you can say, "I run a high-tech business that's disrupting the ____ space." Fill in the blank whether you are in the staffing world, the construction business, a marketing agency, or building homes!

Can you smell the freedom?

Let's Exit By FORCE!

FORCE Exercise: Reflect on your house's automation.

- How do you feel about Cognitive Automation within your business?
- Do you have someone on your team with exposure to automation?
- What is your game plan to execute on the strategy and steps listed above?
- **Weapons: Review the Cognitive Automation Checklist in the Exit By FORCE Toolkit located at ExitByFORCE.com/Weapons**

Notes:

STEP 5: EXPANSION DYNAMICS

One of the last house metaphors, finally! Imagine your business as a home on the market. How did you find your new house? Was it posted on Zillow or Redfin with unbelievable pictures? When you clicked in, did it show you something impressive, like a hidden pool or grand fireplace? When you looked deeper, did you find more interesting information about the house and the larger community that made you want it even more? Of course, like in business, you might select your house based on convenience or proximity to your comforts. But it all started with your ability to *find* the house. That's the same level of appeal we need to create for your business to attract potential buyers. We need to make it easy to find and irresistibly alluring. In this last major section, we will dive into strategies that ensure your business is both visible AND irresistible.

Grand Illusions: Engage the World[45,46,47]

Your digital footprint is often the first impression potential buyers will have of your business. Therefore, it's essential to enhance the website experience to ensure it is modern, user-friendly, and optimized for search engines. This includes implementing strong SEO practices to rank at the top of relevant keyword searches. A well-optimized digital presence increases visibility and establishes a notable presence in the market, much like a well-photographed house listing on Zillow. Ensure your website showcases value clearly and concisely, highlighting key achievements, client testimonials, and case studies to demonstrate your business's strengths. Finally, make sure it has a unique look and feel you are truly proud of. Show your website to friends and family or to the younger generation— what are their thoughts on it? It's your first digital impression; make it look good.

I've worked with many businesses, and surprisingly, many of them go to market without an overhaul of their digital presence. I get it, you want to sell and exit, and you don't want to manage all the additional overhead. Who wants to revamp the content of the website, find someone to design it, and manage the project? Not me, but honestly, it needs to be done. You cannot proclaim that you're a company that uses AI and automation if you have a poor digital presence. Buyers will be skeptical right off the bat. You're at the last step of commanding superior value for your business—don't falter on something that costs a few thousand dollars.

Upgrade your website, ensure it's on the latest versions of the technology stack you chose, ensure it's fully functional for all types of devices and browsers, and make sure every aspect of your website works. Don't lose credibility at this step of the process. Find a great freelancer or reach out to me personally, and I can recommend someone for you to work with. Again, this is your first WOW effect—let's leave it all on the table. At the time of writing this book, the ITTDigital.com website is the one we built to sell the company and could be a good reference point. You can also see how well KenobiCapital.com is designed.

Ensure your social media presence and Google search results yield only the best about your business. I understand that you don't want to suddenly start posting on social media if you haven't so far, but it's honestly very easy and very important to get this done. It shows that the business is modern and thriving, even if it doesn't generate any leads. Acquirers will definitely check your LinkedIn profile and will google you to check company size, revenue, headcount, etc. Google yourself—what comes up? Let's ensure your web presence, blog articles, social media profiles, and any business-listing website show only the best about your business and that they show up at the top! Again, it's better to completely outsource this if you aren't an expert. Reach out for cost-effective freelancers to help you out.

While everything should look focused on generating new business, we are subtly adding characteristics that a buyer would love to see.

Clients—check.

Automation—check.

Brand visibility—check.

Inbound lead generation—check.

Thought leadership—check.

Make sure your digital presence tells your story.

The Art of Perception: Amplifying Your Business Presence

Partnerships are key for brand visibility, especially when you are looking to exit. While partners are mainly developed for strategic sales and referrals, they can be hugely beneficial when selling. Assume you are a Microsoft Gold Partner, which means you work very closely with Microsoft and get the referrals from Microsoft because of all the excellent work you've done for them and their clients. It's something you can highlight across your materials. Now imagine, in passing, that you mention that you are looking to exit at a Microsoft conference or within that partnership ecosystem. Suddenly, any company wanting that specific partnership with Microsoft will look to acquire you because it's a great way for them to build their client database and win business.

It's very interesting to see this dynamic work out. Lawyers, accountants, and bankers are the best at this. Partnerships provide significant value to both generate new business and to highlight the company. Even if business doesn't increase, we should use partnership to position ourselves as a leader in the space.

Another strategy is to secure an industry-recognized certification or form strategic partnerships that can significantly boost your business's credibility and attractiveness to buyers. For example, you could become an Inc. 5000 business, Deloitte Fast 500 or get on the Best Places To Work award. There are hundreds of awards out there, and while they don't normally add too much value, it adds credibility during the exit process, so find one that you qualify for and get it!

Surprisingly, most of these are paid awards and a revenue generator for the publishing business. Even more surprising—people don't know that these awards are paid for so you can easily find one or two awards and get them, as needed. Another option is to set up partnerships with major brands in your industry, like a prominent construction company or a leading hospital system. These affiliations signal to potential buyers that your business meets high standards of quality and reliability, making it a more attractive acquisition target. Don't sweat it too much; we just want to add one or two talking points to emphasize and create web buzz for buyers to validate.

> Spotlights and awards are key aspects to highlight your business. Make sure it's posted all over your digital presence. Have you spoken at a conference or won an award for anything? Again, let's keep in mind your goal to exit. You need to get things done to elevate your digital presence so when you speak to a buyer, you can name-drop these aspects. As an example, I was a *Forbes* Technology Leader years ago. If you google me, it still shows up, and I can introduce myself that way because there are multiple points of credibility. Conferences, spotlights, awards, or any recognition will help elevate your position. Think about how best to position yourself.

Perception plays a crucial role in attracting acquirers. By optimizing your digital presence, forming strategic partnerships, and streamlining operations, you can create the impression of a larger, more established entity. Use professional branding, polished marketing materials, and a strong online presence to project stability and growth potential. Highlight awards, certifications, and notable client logos on your website and become known as a FORCE to be reckoned with.

FORCE Exercise: Reflect on your digital presence.

- Have you revamped or upgraded your digital presence in the last year?
- Does your digital presence subtly speak to buyers, and demonstrate that you're a thought leader to acquire?
- What comes up if you search yourself? Is the data accurate and in good taste?

Notes:

Growth Strategy Unveiled: Your Expansion Dynamics Report

It's surprising how much value a simple report can create. You know your business the best—the good, the bad, and the ugly. You probably have a hundred ideas on how to improve your business and generate new business. You know the areas of untapped potential. Let's use that to your advantage.

You should show a potential buyer how they can get a return on investment (ROI) quickly by taking a few actions that you don't have the bandwidth to address. You can address expansion within current accounts with the addition of sales efforts or experts, new capabilities that can be cross-sold within existing accounts, and partnerships and referral programs that could be implemented to increase leads. Further, the buyer could leverage the company to be the low-cost delivery wing for a larger company or go after more partnership tiers or certifications that will position the business better. This report should be thorough and comprehensive, so the buyer understands the actions to take to get a wonderful ROI.

Think about all the talking points you'll have once you complete this exercise. You'll be able to showcase to your future buyer exactly what they stand to gain once they implement your ideas—a surefire way to bring about a successful sale!

The Grand Finale: Bringing It All Together

Notice that during this entire section I didn't mention anything about actually winning new clients. If there is an opportunity for new clients, your organization is well-positioned to win it. While additional revenue would be a fantastic reward for these efforts, you must maintain focus on selling your business; showcasing how attractive your business really is and making it extremely desirable for buyers. When we talk about Expansion Dynamics, we look to show buyers that everything is in place for them to elevate the company to the next level.

Whether buyers are looking for a strategic acquisition because you bring a unique skill set or a bolt-on acquisition because of your revenue and logos, it's important to showcase yourself in the best light possible. You want to control the entire exit process and be the irresistible addition to their strategy.

By focusing on these key areas, you ensure that your business isn't just a blip on the radar but a beacon of opportunity. Each step you take in optimizing your digital presence, engaging on social media, leveraging analytics, and building relationships adds layers of value and attractiveness. You're not just selling a business; you're presenting a well-oiled, future-ready enterprise that can take on new challenges and opportunities.

Great job on getting your business ready to Exit By FORCE. You're now in the best shape of your life! You look good, you feel good, and you're ready to tackle the world. Congratulations on getting here; you can almost touch freedom!

Now, it's time to actually exit and Maximize Founder Value under the most favorable terms.

Let's Exit By FORCE!

FORCE Exercise: Reflect on your house's visibility.

- How do you feel about Expansion Dynamics within your business?

- Are you happy with your digital presence, social media, and the organization's reach?

- What is your game plan to execute on the strategy and steps listed above?

- **Weapons: Review the Expansion Dynamics Checklist in the Exit By FORCE Toolkit located at ExitByFORCE.com/Weapons**

Notes:

SUMMARY: FORCE UNLEASHED

I've given you the FORCE methodology to Maximize Founder Value. You will see companies exit that are following this formula across your network. These are the companies exiting under the most favorable terms and controlling the narrative. They are Exiting By FORCE instead of letting someone else control their destiny and generational wealth.

When the stakes are high, always be in control!

The by-product of following the steps outlined in this book is that, regardless of selling, you will now have an extremely well-run organization. Even if you choose not to exit or decide to keep your business after implementing these strategies, your business will transform into a success story with clarity, credibility, and profitability.

Over the next twelve months, I can guarantee you that my inbox will be full of people sending success stories as a result of following the FORCE framework. I already know what they will say. Their emails will tell me about the work they put in to implement these strategies, how they used the free Weapons available to them at ExitByFORCE.com and got the best deal they could imagine. They will next be asking me how to manage their millions of dollars of generational wealth as they figure out what to do with their new-found freedom. They will tell me that the rewards paid off and that the journey itself was fun and exciting.

They will tell me that they experienced big benefits after doing the work set out in this book:

- They had a multimillion-dollar exit where buyers were fighting over their business.
- They've managed to sell at a value higher than expected.
- They controlled the terms of negotiation and the destiny of the business.
- They are ready to sail into the sunset after a successful journey, where their family and friends are proud of them!
- They've profited so much additional wealth that they're setting up trust funds, not only for their own children, but their nieces and nephews and godchildren as well.

One client will even say he's planning to take a year-long cruise and gamble his savings away; to which I will say, "To each their own!"

I sincerely want you to be in this group and email me your story, telling me you have done these five steps and made yourself more wealth than you expected along the way.

Sadly, there's a good chance you won't be. People can get addicted to struggle, and let complexity and unimportant actions get in the way. As time passes by, many people will drop this as a priority and lose control of their destiny for a few immediate quick wins.

Over the years, I've founded, scaled, bought, and sold businesses as an entrepreneur and an owner/operator. I've seen my network go through ebbs and flows, and I've had a front row seat to how people make decisions and take actions for their business and their life.

In Episode 3 of this book, I'll share the tips and tricks of highly successful people, people who implemented this process successfully and Maximized Founder Value versus those who get caught in the storm of life. The last Episode will offer ideas on how to overcome these obstacles and Exit By FORCE without the struggles so many people face. It's time to bring it all together, as friends.

Trust in the FORCE!

3

YOUR FOCUS DETERMINES YOUR REALITY

The final steps of your journey to a successful business exit require clarity, determination, and a focused mindset.

In this episode, you'll learn how to harness the power of focus to align your actions with your goals, ensuring that every decision and effort moves you closer to your desired outcome. By concentrating on the most impactful actions and maintaining a laser-sharp focus on your objectives, you'll shape the reality you envision for your business and your future.

Remember, your focus determines your reality—stay committed, stay driven, and let the FORCE guide you to your ultimate success.

FIRST-TIME SELLERS ARE EXCITED TO CASH IN ON THEIR SUCCESS

There's a predictable journey that you will go through to pursue a wonderful exit experience with success, a sense of accomplishment, and no regrets. There are usually four types of small business exits: explorers, agent-based sellers, desperate sellers, and those that Exit By FORCE.

Explorer sellers are business owners who are open to emails and phone calls about their business. They are super enthusiastic and want to see what's out there. "What's my business really worth?" These business owners are usually willing to put in hard work, taking introductory calls and answering questions about their business. They aren't too concerned about it moving to the next stage, and often most of the conversations don't move forward. They are not well-prepared to sell and do not have all the documentation required; once a buyer asks for information, the business owner drags their feet, and the deal falls through. If the owner does have a few details, they're usually not presented in a manner that the buyer wants, and the back and forth kills the deal. They put in a lot of time for very little reward and hope that someone will give them an offer based on the limited information available. Even when they do sell, it's a nominal amount with less-than-ideal profits.

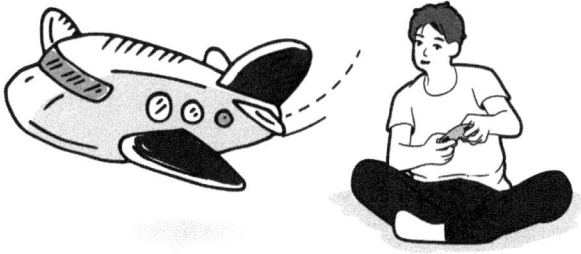

Agent-based sellers are business owners who decide to sell their business, and the first thing they do is look for a broker to represent them. These owners, unfortunately, have not done their research on business brokers. Business brokers have not run your business or a business in your industry; they don't understand the value you bring to the table and cannot advise you on how to stage your business to Maximize Founder Value. All they want to do is sign up businesses and collect a fee or take those businesses off the market in the off chance that someone buys them. They usually lock the business owner into a six-month or one-year contract and do very little work to actually market the business. They also charge exorbitant fees.

Why would you donate 8%–10% or some complex pricing model percentage of your business to a real estate agent? You built this business with blood, sweat, and years, so if they don't bring the value from $5 million to $8 million, what are they being paid for? We are used to paying real estate fees and think this is normal, but it's not. We should only pay advisers that increase our value and overall net an increased amount of money in our pockets. The broker's incentives don't align with small business owners, and the owners usually feel manipulated, dissatisfied, and overall unhappy about the business sale, if it even sells. The broker's business model is to have as much inventory as possible in hopes that someone will buy one of the companies. They don't control the business's destiny and do not care about your well-being—and it shows.

Desperate sellers are business owners who have, unfortunately, been unable to secure a deal to their liking. Despite interest from various buyers, no one seems genuinely interested in purchasing the business. The owner, not having staged the business for sale, might end up selling for a nominal amount or shutting down entirely, an unfortunate end to their journey and their dreams. These businesses sell for pennies or close down, reflecting a worst-case scenario. Unfortunately, as discussed in Episode 1, nine out of ten businesses fall into this category. I've seen many of these businesses sell for $1, and I've seen a few of my friends buy these businesses, use the Exit By FORCE framework, and turn them around and sell for millions of dollars within a year. Don't be a desperate seller.

Finally, you have the giant exits with dollar bills floating everywhere—these are business owners that **Exit By FORCE**. They apply the FORCE principles flawlessly and make it look easy. They will have to work for it, as I'm sure you've surmised, but they always have multiple buyers inquiring about the business and can negotiate the most favorable terms for the outcomes they are looking for. Their inbox is full of opportunities, and they have a full data room and suite of tools ready for anyone to evaluate the business. **If you haven't already, open up your arsenal and get a free financial audit of your business. You can find this resource at ExitByFORCE.com/Weapons.** The value of the business increases quickly when word spreads that someone is looking to buy, and with a few phone calls, magic can happen.

The Exit By FORCE business owner controls their destiny, they control the exit process, they control the negotiation, and they are free to walk away anytime if they choose to pursue another path. They Exit By FORCE; not by accident, not for pennies, and not without control.

When the stakes are high, always be in control!

FORCE Exercise: Reflect on your small business exit category, and be completely honest with yourself.

- Where are you in the exit process and what actions have you taken so far?
- How do you want your business staged for an exit?
- What is your game plan to Exit By FORCE?
- **Weapons: Get a free financial audit of your business located at ExitByFORCE.com/Weapons**

Notes:

FINESSING THE EXIT MINEFIELD

This dynamic among small business owners creates a predictable phenomenon. Explorers, after speaking to many potential acquirers, soon realize the process is much harder than anticipated. They turn to brokers or M&A advisors who promise them the moon and sign them up into long-term agreements. These brokers, however, are vendors, not true partners, and often add no real value to the business or the exit experience. The business ends up as inventory to the broker, who has a history of taking advantage of small business owners. As the owner becomes desperate, unable to sell, checked out of the business, and already spending money the broker foretold would come, they soon realize the broker made unrealistic promises.

Finally, the broker contract ends, and the business owner is desperate to sell to anyone. They finally sell to a buyer who knows the game and includes numerous clauses and downside protections to safeguard the buyer's investment. This buyer eventually walks away with the company for far less than the original deal value due to the stipulations in place. Unfortunately, they know how to play the game too!

The owner ends up with a terrible exit experience and begins to resent the company they built. This isn't a one-time occurrence; it happens time and again, and every business owner is *confident* it won't happen to them—until it does. Don't let yourself get into this predicament.

Whether you are an explorer, signed up with a broker, or in a desperate position, having come so far into this book you know what the solution is. The principles in this book explain how to avoid falling into the trap that consumes nine out of ten small businesses. It's not going to happen overnight, we know that. It's going to take some hard work and dedication. But ultimately what you'll gain will be oh so sweet.

Since I'm a Harry Potter buff, I'll give you a quick analogy. The sixth Harry Potter book begins in the Prime Minister's office. The PM is aware of wizards in the story, and has regular correspondence with the Minister for Magic in the magical world. When the Minister for Magic drops into the PM's office to tell him that Voldemort has returned to power, and that the "good" side, along with Harry Potter, are doing everything they can to fight him off, the PM gets flustered and asks a question: 'But for heaven's sake – you're wizards ! You can do magic ! Surely you can sort out – well – anything !' To which, the Minister for Magic says, 'The trouble is, the other side can do magic too, Prime Minister.'[48]

The buyers, in most cases, know what they're doing. They have a plethora of trusted advisors at their disposal. They're typically not new to this, and they're not coming in blind. If they recognize your lack of experience, and you have no guidance either, they'll eat you alive. I'm telling you this because I want you to be realistic. Take the time to do your homework and find a partner you trust to help guide you through the minefield. Kenobi Capital, for example, has an excellent accelerator called Exit By FORCE that simplifies a majority of the steps listed in this book to help get you to where you need to be in record time. Take the time to explore other companies like ours to find one that truly resonates with you and makes you feel safe. Reach out to me if you'd like a list of questions you can ask potential partners to vet them. Both you and your partner company need to feel like it's a good fit for it to really work.

> Resist the temptation to list your business until you have applied this methodology and can control the exit process. Answer this question: what is peace of mind worth to you?

You know how everyone talks about a person or company that sold for tens of millions of dollars and becomes an overnight success? You can be that business owner and that company. You can become the talk of the town. Get ready for the interviews and the paparazzi once you Exit By FORCE.

Remember, Your Focus Determines Your Reality.

FORCE Exercise: Reflect on shared and aligned incentives when working with others.

- Have you worked with a consultant or advisor that you feel didn't have your best interest at heart or couldn't relate to you?

- Do you have someone in your network with an exit experience that you can trust, and is aligned with your best interests?

- Have you thought about your identity post exit? Can interviews and publicity of a successful exit get you there?

Notes:

HOUSTON, START THE COUNTDOWN TO FREEDOM

The process of selling your business takes time, and it's natural to think about FREEDOM. When will you get the freedom to choose a new path? For many of us, once we decide to sell, a weight lifts off our shoulders. We no longer need to focus on growing the business, adding clients, delivering projects, or hiring people. Instead, we switch gears to ensure the machine runs smoothly as we prepare for the sale. However, making the decision to sell doesn't mean you're free just yet. You still have to get the business ready for sale.

Your creation has been running based on your wants and needs over many years, but does it cater to someone else's aspirations or story? Do they have the same type of household or philosophy as you, or maybe special needs that must be accommodated before they move in? As small business owners, we feel our business is the greatest thing since sliced bread, and we rightfully should because our business feels like very little risk to us. A buyer, however, sees tremendous risk as they are paying the most important employee of the company a lot of money to walk away from the business. I wouldn't pay my second-in-command a ton of money and say, "Please leave." Would you?

I can't speak to other frameworks, but I know the FORCE framework like the back of my hand. So let's pretend you've made the decision to implement it. This method can be implemented within two quarters if it's your sole focus, but the results will take time to materialize. Once implemented, the financial house will magically change, and you'll see the business creating profits you didn't expect. And with profits, the value goes up.

You want at least six months of clean books before hitting the market so that you can proudly showcase the trend as the current standing of your business. With six months of financials clear of personal expenses and operating with reduced working capital, you can Maximize Founder Value.

Second, once the house is staged and ready for the market, you should give yourself adequate time to negotiate and get the most favorable offer. Businesses that want to sell immediately will leave money on the table, as negotiators on the other side are in no rush and will drag out the process in hopes of getting a better deal.

You should expect another six months to negotiate and ensure that buyers reach deep into their piggy bank to make the deal go through. Remember, you are highly desirable after implementing the FORCE framework, and there are not many companies like yours on the market. Command that higher price point and take your time. You are not here to settle at the very end.

Last, you need to de-risk the deal for the buyer and consider how long you can stay on to transition the business. The longer you are willing to stay on as a consultant or employee, the higher the chance your business will be acquired. Most buyers will require a one- or two-year employment agreement. There are ways to get around this during deal negotiation, but you should consider some transition time as part of the process to sell your business.

This entire process can take you well over two years when done properly and done by yourself. This will probably feel like an eternity once you've decided to sell, and it is a realistic timeline if you choose to go it alone.

FORCE Exercise: Reflect on your timeline to freedom.

- Have you made the decision to get the business ready for an exit? Is the weight lifted off your shoulders?
- What is your ideal timeline to exit considering the FORCE principles, buyer conversations, and transition time?
- How do you plan to achieve this timeline? Are there options to reduce the workload and shorten the timeline?

Notes:

CUTTING CORNERS CAN COST YOU MILLIONS

"But Anand, I don't want to work for another two years!" I've heard this countless times while helping small business owners through the exit process. And I agree—I don't want to work forever when it's time to sail into the sunset. That's the power of best practices. Unfortunately, business owners who tackle this alone often fail because they fall into a trial-and-error process and get discouraged due to costly mistakes. It's very easy to procrastinate when you don't know where to start or lack a capable team to execute this framework tirelessly. You may even, unknowingly, take actions that damage your life's hard work.

For example, you might choose to overhaul the brand messaging, assuming that's what buyers expect, or implement a new finance/accounting system without understanding how it affects the rest of the business operations. You may even change the reason why someone finds you attractive in the first place. These errors will set you back; time is money!

Without the right guidance and understanding of best practices, it's easy to under budget and overcommit to the exit process. This process will cost you money, and we don't want to put that investment in the wrong place or harm the business in any way.

Obviously, this happens because you haven't sold a business before—you only sell once, and if you're lucky enough, you sell twice. Business owners are often unaware of the best practices to sell their business. In every industry, there are best practices to apply, and it's crucial to follow them, understand them, and execute with a sense of urgency. These practices evolve over time. We used to sell businesses in newspapers and through brokers, and now we can list them for free (BizBuySell, Smergers, Biz-Quest, BusinessesForSale, etc.) just like we self-list houses.

I'm sure the exit process will continue to evolve with AI and future technology, and it's important to stay up-to-date with current trends and best practices. It's also important to allocate a budget to the exit process. If invested in the right place, this will generate tremendous returns. The team at Exit By FORCE actually returns your money at the exit—now that's pretty cool!

During my first sale, we didn't invest the necessary budget. We cut corners on advisors and legal experts and thought we could do it all by ourselves. This led to a brutal, heart-wrenching, three-year lawsuit for the owners, family members, and stakeholders. We ended up spending over half a million dollars (the exit value was in the tens of millions), switching between multiple legal firms, and taking on debt. As of 2024, we are still waiting to receive the entire settlement funds for an exit that happened in 2020!

Finally, we won! The private equity company that bought us had done it to others before and settled to pay out the entire sum of money owed to us. While I cannot speak on the exact settlement details, we are getting our money, and that's what counts: money and peace of mind!

It's vital to dedicate a budget to this process and partner with someone who has aligned incentives and genuinely wants you to be successful. Someone who's been in your shoes before and empathizes with your situation. You don't want to end up in a lawsuit and hate the business you've built with blood, sweat, and years. Trust me, I've clearly learned the hard way. What I wouldn't give for that peace of mind and security that I would have had if it had all gone smoothly in 2020.

This exit cost us millions of dollars in time and money—not to forget the reputation hit with shareholders, employees, and the broader network. Imagine being in this position; it sucks! Choose wisely. You're at the end of your journey. Don't screw it up, and don't cut corners. There is no need to when you are running a cash-generating enterprise.

FORCE Exercise: Reflect on your exit budget.

- Have you thought about your investment in the exit process?
- Do you know the best practices for exits in your industry?
- What is peace of mind worth to you?

Notes:

DREAM TEAM, ASSEMBLE!

The top assets of your business are your people. Building a business is a team activity, and millionaires and billionaires rely on their teams to help them every day! Apple wasn't only successful because of its visionary, Steve Jobs, but also because he had a fantastic COO named Tim Cook. Tim Cook executed the vision relentlessly with strong processes, best practices, and a fantastic team.[1,2,3] You are the visionary of your business, and now, at the time of your exit, it's time for you to get your execution team in place.

Leverage your network. Look for those who have exited before and ask for help. Can you find a fabulous finance or operations person who you can trust to join your team? There's a huge advantage to learning from people who have gone before you, especially when you need help executing on so many fronts (finance, operations, resources, automation, etc.) simultaneously. Hiring individuals for each area could be expensive, so we need a better game plan to execute across the board.

I'm always surprised when I hear an owner say they want to do it on their own, and I always ask them why they want to go through the struggle. There is always someone who has made the same mistake before us, and it's better we learn from their journey. While we, as small business owners, feel that our journey is unique, there are millions of us going through the entrepreneurial journey who face the exact same situations. The journey of small business growth and exits is actually extremely predictable, and everyone goes through the same set of scenarios. Sometimes we don't like to share our wins and challenges, but I promise you, the next guy or gal has the exact same wins and challenges. We are in a digital world, so it's easy to connect with someone and learn from their mistakes.

Stay focused. When left alone, most people get distracted, and the exit process could take a back seat as client deliveries are at stake or something else comes up. It's easy to get uninspired and offtrack without quick wins and a dopamine hit. To ensure you realize the Exit By FORCE potential and get the outcomes you deserve, it's important to find a way to stay on track, whether that's advisors, an accountability circle, or a partner.

Your Focus Determines Your Reality!

Left to our own devices, we never truly achieve our full potential. Most large companies have co-founders to keep each other on track, and investors won't even consider companies founded by a single person. You need co-founders, a team, advisors, and coaches to be successful. You need a partner aligned with your incentives, with the goal of Maximizing Founder Value, your generational wealth, and doing it under the most favorable terms. Try to find a partner who can help you with all the areas of the FORCE framework, almost a one-stop shop that can put it all together for you while you focus on what's important—running your business.

Invest wisely. Owners who are struggling often hate to pay for help and try to do everything themselves. They design their own logo, set up their website, try to host it themselves, all while setting up the business finances. It's tough to be both a finance expert and a digital design expert. While this book gives you the focus areas to do it on your own, this is one of the most important things you are going to do in your life. Do you really want to do it alone, when you haven't done it before? You need experts. This is about selling YOUR business, YOUR life's work.

People who are high achievers surround themselves with visionaries and experts who can help in various aspects of their business. Leverage your network, leverage advisors, and don't risk making painful mistakes, especially in the most important part of your journey. You're on the final mile of the marathon—don't trip! Make sure your team of experts can do this faster, cheaper, and smarter and get you over the finish line, safely, with millions of dollars in your pocket. You have a successful business generating positive cash flow—invest it in YOUR exit process.

The Exit By FORCE team works with a select few companies each year where we can increase value immensely. Book a free Exit Strategy Session to answer your questions and learn more at ExitByFORCE.com/Weapons.

Be cautious of those not aligned with your best interests. Traditional brokers, investment bankers, and M&A advisors may not always have incentives that align with yours. They could even prolong the process to keep charging you fees. You want to get the deal done efficiently, so ensure your team is aligned with you and not just collecting an hourly rate. Make sure to partner with those who have a track record of success in small business exits and share your goals of Maximizing Founder Value under the most favorable terms.

FORCE Exercise: Reflect on your exit team.

- Have you thought about who you can leverage to help you along the exit process?
- Do you have experts to help attack on all fronts simultaneously?
- How will you keep yourself focused on the exit journey?
- **Weapons: Book an Exit Strategy Session at ExitByFORCE.com/Weapons**

Notes:

AN OBJECT IN MOTION STAYS IN MOTION

Many owners wait for the "right" time to act, but this mentality rarely works when selling a business, as life is always busy. Think about when you were planning for kids, or if you haven't yet, imagine what it will be like. Is there ever a perfect time when life just gives you some downtime? Never, and it's easy to be non-committal and make excuses. The time is now—let's commit to closing this out with a bang.

The winners and losers in the exit game are predictable. Successful exits come to those who commit to the process and take action to create forward momentum. Once the initial inertia is broken, the process will take care of itself. Those who struggle, get distracted easily, and don't have someone to hold them account-able will always prioritize something urgent instead of something important. Important actions create value.

Think about how you started your entrepreneurial journey and the quick actions you took right away. You had an idea, started talking to customers, quickly incorporated, and just started figuring it out. When the first invoice was to be issued, you made it happen. When the first expense came in, you got a credit card and made it happen. Think about what would have happened if you hadn't done this—you wouldn't have built a wonderful business, generational wealth for your family, and become the hero you are today. It's all about that forward momentum.

So pick yourself up by your bootstraps and keep chugging along. It's time to make it happen. Don't delay. Jump into the FORCE principles, get your team together, and start executing your exit strategy.

Trying these strategies has no downside for you or the business. It can only help you on your way to success. It's a small experiment or initiative you are trying as a business owner. You have hired many people in your business life—some were fantastic, and some were duds. You still risked hiring because the positives outweighed the negatives when you got a great hire. The same applies here.

With the ideas in this book, I'm asking you to put thought into how a buyer views your company. Even better, think about how you view another business when you first look at it, and how you would approach buying a company. These actions take time, and you might need to invest and get guidance along the way. The framework in this book allows you to test the principles in a risk-free way and see how they can improve your business results.

Once you are ready, you can start making small investments to accelerate your Exit By FORCE and Maximize Founder Value under the most favorable terms.

Become one of the most desirable, valuable, and efficient businesses to acquire in your industry. The upside is unlimited!

Get ready.

Get set.

GO.

YOUR LEGACY WILL ECHO THROUGH THE GALAXY

A note from the author, Anand Narayan.

Hey, Business Owner,

Congratulations on making it through this book—that was a LOT of information, and I applaud you for getting to the very end. It may feel like we've only just scratched the surface, but you actually are in a far better place now than before you picked this book up. It just doesn't feel that way yet.

Remember, you've created something extraordinary, and there are not many businesses like yours. Once staged with these principles, you will be irresistible. This is honestly one of the most important things you will ever do to set yourself and your future generations up for success. You've taken massive risks, avoided conventional wisdom, broken societal rules, and created something wonderful. Don't feel bad about milking it. Remember, there are experts on the other side of the table. Don't give them any rope; they want YOU. Play hard to get, and control your journey.

If you take away anything from this book, make sure you cover your bases. Peace of mind is irrelevant until you lose it, and then there is nothing you wouldn't do to get it back. I hope you've learned from the mistakes I've made and find immense success. As a small business owner myself, I'm on your team, aligned with your goals, here as a guide, and wishing you the very best. You got this!

I'm super excited to hear about your journey and how this book assisted in your exit. Whether you are doing $2 million or $20 million makes no difference to me! Please reach out to me via any channel you choose. The afterword has my details. I would love to hear your success story, and hope it inspires others too. I would also love to hear of new challenges you may have faced so we can continue to protect small business owners and entrepreneurs across the globe.

Your inner circle must be very proud of you; they know the sacrifices you've made. I've always been extremely proud of my father, who immigrated to the United States, built a highly successful business, sold it for eight figures, and lived the American dream from rags to riches. Even if your family and friends might not vocalize it, trust me, they are proud!

Years from now, after your wonderful exit, no one will remember the beginning or the middle, but they will remember the end, your exit, and how you put the family on the map. They will tell tall tales about you, passed on through the years, embellished with each generation, of your journey and how you walked a hero's path.

The Path You Choose Is Yours Alone. Trust In The FORCE. Your focus determines your reality. Stay committed, stay focused, and stay hungry. The future is bright, and the opportunities are endless. Thank you for joining me on this journey and joining the elite who Exit By FORCE.

Sincerely,

Anand Narayan

Anand Narayan

AFTERWORD: TOOLS FOR SUCCESS

To continue your journey and help you along the way, make use of the Weapons available to you at ExitByFORCE.com/Weapons.

They are free and will guide you on the path to glory. This wealth of information will be updated many times each year to publish the latest and greatest news for small businesses owners, so ensure to check back in and see if there is a new Weapon available in your arsenal and at your disposal.

Please don't be a stranger. I would love to hear your story! I'm sure you will successfully implement these strategies, use the free Weapons available at ExitByFORCE.com and get the deal of a lifetime.

I hope you tell me that:

- You had a multimillion-dollar exit where buyers were fighting over your business, achieving a value higher than expected.
- You controlled the terms of negotiation and the destiny of the business you've built over many years.
- You are ready to sail into the sunset, after a successful journey, with a proud and inspired set of family and friends.

If you ever need any help along the way, please reach out to me. Just make sure to say Exit By FORCE in the message!

LinkedIn:https://www.linkedin.com/in/anandnarayan-kenobicapital/
Email: Anand@kenobicapital.com
Text/WhatsApp: +1.732.501.0586
Calendly: https://calendly.com/anandkenobicapital

Remember, the journey to a successful exit is not one you have to take alone. With the right team, the right strategies, and the right mindset, you can achieve the exit of your dreams and set yourself up for the next chapter of your life.

When the stakes are high, always be in control!

THE EXIT BY FORCE ACCELERATOR

The Exit By FORCE accelerator is a forty-week program tailored for companies based in the United States. We welcome a hundred businesses annually seeking to Maximize Founder Value under the most favorable terms.

Upon joining the accelerator program, businesses gain numerous opportunities to exit or may continue operations with heightened efficiency. Our team becomes an integral extension of your company and aligns its incentives with yours.

Should you choose to exit independently post-accelerator program, we extend our best wishes for your success.

Alternatively, you can choose to exit with us to capital markets and receive a **full refund** on your investment.

Our commitment is to align with small business owners and offer maximum flexibility throughout the exit process.

We believe that the environment shapes performance; thus, we have cultivated conditions conducive to achieving rapid results.

Our team comprises founders, owners/operators, millionaires, and world-class experts dedicated to driving your success.

Learn more at KenobiCapital.com

When you look closely, you'll notice businesses across all industries adopting this strategy to position themselves as appealing acquisition targets and secure exits on their own terms. This approach doesn't require years of effort, luck, or hard work. It's about concentrating on the most impactful actions that make your company the most desirable option within your industry.

ABOUT ANAND NARAYAN

Anand is the founder and owner/operator of multiple small businesses. His exposure to entrepreneurship began early, as his father started IT Trailblazers when Anand was just nine years old. After being honorably discharged from the Navy, Anand joined his father and helped grow the company to $65 million in revenue before successfully exiting. Following this, he earned his MBA from Cornell University and co-founded ITTDigital with his father, scaling the business to $10 million and exiting within three years. Both exits provided vastly different experiences and stories, enriching Anand's expertise.

Anand's goal is to help small business owners worldwide Maximize Founder Value. The exit of IT Trailblazers resulted in a grueling three-year lawsuit that the founding family eventually won. This experience drives Anand's mission to ensure that no founder has to endure a similar ordeal. He is dedicated to helping founders exit on their own terms, celebrating the businesses they've built with their blood, sweat, and years of hard work.

In addition to his business ventures, Anand is a strong advocate for personal finance. Taught by his mother, a Wall Street banker, Anand leverages his knowledge to help his network, friends, and family invest effectively, aiming for financial growth without incurring asset management fees. With much of America in debt and the future uncertain, he believes personal finance is the key to achieving financial freedom and generational wealth.

Today, Anand runs Kenobi Capital, a firm dedicated to helping small business owners exit with peace of mind, ensuring they are doing the best for their business and family. He is selective about the businesses he works with, ensuring his team elevates their valuation. Anand is a champion for the little guys, supporting those who break societal norms, take risks, and build value.

An avid Star Wars fan, Anand wishes you: May The FORCE Be With You.

MORE PRAISE FOR EXIT BY FORCE

In my career leading global high-technology businesses, driving innovation, and executing successful market strategies, I've learned the importance of strategic preparation for growth and exit. Anand Narayan's Exit By FORCE framework is a powerful tool for business leaders seeking to maximize value and achieve successful exits. His approach, which aligns operational excellence with strategic foresight, offers the clarity needed to turn organizational strengths into compelling opportunities for buyers. This book is an invaluable resource for any leader focused on profitable growth and a successful exit.

— Sudhakar Raman, SVP & General Manager at FormFactor
and Former COO of SVXR

As a founder, we often focus on building a business and driving growth, but planning an exit strategy from the start is rarely discussed in depth. This is why "EXIT BY FORCE" is such a unique, timely, and essential guide. When talking to Anand and learning about his FORCE framework, this was an eye-opener for me. If you're looking to maximize your business's valuation for a successful exit, this book is for you. It provides a practical, step-by-step approach to navigating the complexities of an exit strategy.

— Nam Phong Ho,
Entrepreneur and Founder

Anand Narayan's Exit By FORCE is a game-changer for business owners looking to navigate the complex world of business exits. Anand brilliantly shifts the perspective from merely running a business to strategically building one that is a valuable, irresistible product for potential buyers. He not only addresses the operational side but also dives into the psychology of what makes a business attractive for acquisition. This is essential reading for any entrepreneur serious about maximizing the value of their hard work.

— Tibor Dudjik - Entrepreneur / Fractional COO / Board Member

Anand Narayan's Exit By FORCE is a must-read for entrepreneurs and investors in the healthtech space. Having transitioned from a physician and entrepreneur to a venture capitalist, I understand the importance of strategic planning and execution for successful exits. Anand's framework provides actionable insights that resonate deeply with the challenges and opportunities we face in the rapidly evolving healthcare industry. This book is a valuable resource for those looking to scale and exit with maximum impact.

— Julien L. Pham, MD, MPH, Founder & Managing Partner at 3CC | Third Culture Capital

Exit By FORCE is a refreshing and insightful read for any business owner thinking about their next big step. Anand Narayan's ability to bust common myths, like the idea that effort automatically equals value, was an eye-opener for me. He gently nudges you to understand that getting your business ready "just in time" is a risky gamble—something I hadn't fully grasped before reading this book.

What really sets this book apart is Anand's blend of practical advice with a touch of humor. His personal experiences, shared with a down-to-earth tone, make the journey of exit planning feel both achievable and even enjoyable. His clear, metaphor-rich writing not only simplifies complex concepts but also leaves you feeling inspired and ready to take action.

Whether you're years away from selling your business or just starting to consider it, Exit By FORCE offers valuable insights and a good laugh along the way. It's like getting advice from a knowledgeable friend who's been there and done that—and wants to see you succeed too.

— Debbie Jenkins, Entrepreneur, Author and Publisher

In 'Exit By FORCE,' Anand Narayan delivers an indispensable guide for any entrepreneur contemplating the intricacies of business sales. With his compelling narrative and hands-on approach, Narayan dismantles common myths about exiting a business and introduces the revolutionary FORCE methodology. This book isn't just about selling your business—it's about mastering the art of the exit. Narayan shares his transformative journey with authenticity, offering readers the tools to achieve financial optimization, operational excellence, and resource maximization. This isn't just a read; it's a roadmap to ensuring that you do so with confidence, control, and maximum value when ready to exit. A must-read for those who refuse to leave their future to chance.

— Indira Bunic, Non-Executive Director, CEO, & Leadership Expert with a focus on Strategy, Governance, & Marketing

As a leader in legal operations and M&A, I know the importance of being legally prepared for a business exit. Anand Narayan's Exit By FORCE offers a comprehensive framework that not only ensures the legal bases are covered but also provides the peace of mind that comes from knowing your business is truly ready for a successful transition. His methodical approach to aligning legal readiness with strategic goals is a game-changer for anyone looking to exit with confidence.

— Matias Toye, Senior Legal Operations Leader and M&A Expert. Founder of Oyster Shield.

Anand does an excellent job of explaining the nuances of running a business so it is attractive to buyers. This book really should be called "How To Sell Your Business for Dummies" because it simplifies the complexity of what is required without diluting the important information. He lays out the concepts so they are easy to understand, which makes it is easy to implement, which means that a business owner can substantially increase the valuation of their business. This book is a must read for all business owners who want to be prepared in the event the opportunity arises for an exit!

— Janelle Sam, Chief Executive Officer of Seabrook Law Offices

Exit by Force offers profound insights into the strategic nuances of business exits. Its Five-Step Method provides clear, actionable strategies for increasing company valuation, streamlining operations, and leveraging modern technologies. The book simplifies complex financial concepts, making them accessible and highly practical, even for creative entrepreneurs without a deep finance background. It's a must-read for any business owner aiming to create lasting value and strategically position their brand for a successful acquisition.

— Snigdha Yedla,
Founder & Chief Executive Officer at Mann Sey

Exit By FORCE is a must-read for all entrepreneurs, especially those considering their first exit. Anand Narayan provides invaluable, first-hand insight into maximizing exit value and strategically preparing for a successful sale. The book is packed with actionable information and real-world strategies that will resonate with any business owner looking to achieve the most favorable terms. It's a page-turner full of powerful knowledge, making it essential reading for anyone serious about optimizing their exit process.

— Yohei Shimasaki,
Chief Financial Officer at ClimeCo, CPA

EXIT BY FORCE was an easy, digestible read jam-packed with personal examples, actionable insights, and important lessons learned. Anand Narayan clearly has the small business owner's success at the forefront of his mind and his work. It's nice to see a book truly focused on the little guy from someone who's walked that path. I highly recommend!

– Alexis Duclos,
Chief Operations Officer at Kenobi Capital

The captivating opening episode, titled "Learner to Master", is worthy of a paperback bestselling fiction. It immediately captures the reader's attention with a gripping personal anecdote that serves as a powerful metaphor for the central theme: the importance of maintaining control when the stakes are high. The author effectively transitions from a near-disastrous flight experience to the world of business, underscoring the critical lesson that applies to both life and entrepreneurship—never relinquish control, especially when it comes to your business and wealth. This introduction sets the stage for what promises to be a highly practical and insightful guide for small business owners contemplating an exit. The author's candid recounting of his own experiences—one fraught with mistakes and near loss, the other a well-planned and successful exit—provides a relatable and authentic foundation for the advice that follows. This authenticity is one of the section's strongest points; the author doesn't just preach principles but shares hard-earned lessons, making the content both credible and engaging. The standout feature of this section is its emphasis on the emotional and personal aspects of selling a business. The author acknowledges that exiting a business is not just a financial transaction but a deeply personal journey that affects not just the business owner but their family and stakeholders. This holistic approach adds depth to the narrative and makes the book relevant to a broader audience. This teaser effectively builds anticipation for the following chapters, but some readers might wish for a bit more substance upfront to fully grasp what the methodology entails.

The next episode of the book, titled "Trust In The FORCE," is a compelling and actionable guide for business owners looking to optimize their companies for a successful exit. The author effectively introduces the FORCE methodology, a structured framework that provides clear, strategic steps to make a business an irresistible acquisition target. One of the strengths of this episode is its use of the "staged house" metaphor, which simplifies the concept of preparing a business for sale. By comparing the process to staging a house for potential buyers, the author makes the sometimes daunting task of business optimization more relatable and easier to understand. This metaphor is particularly effective in breaking down the five key elements of the FORCE methodology—Financial Optimization, Operational Excellence, Resource Maximization, Cognitive Automation, and Expansion Dynamics. Each element is explained in a way that highlights its importance and provides actionable insights for implementation. However, the episode is not just about theory; it encourages readers to actively engage with the content through reflective exercises. These exercises prompt business owners to assess their current standing in each of the FORCE areas, making the advice more interactive and applicable to their specific situations. This approach not only enhances the reader's understanding but also motivates them to take immediate action. Overall, Episode 2 is a well-crafted, insightful, and practical section of the book. It successfully balances theory with actionable advice, making it an invaluable resource for business owners preparing for a sale. The FORCE methodology is presented as a powerful tool, and the author's confidence in its effectiveness is contagious. This episode is likely to leave readers feeling empowered and ready to take control of their exit strategy, trusting in the FORCE to guide them to a successful outcome.

In my review of this episode, me opinion on the various steps that constitute the FORCE is as below:

Step 1: Financial Optimization is a well-structured and insightful section that offers practical guidance for business owners preparing to sell their businesses. The author effectively uses the metaphor of staging a house to make the complex process of financial optimization more relatable and understandable, emphasizing that first impressions are crucial when presenting a business to potential buyers. One of the strengths of this section is its practical, actionable advice. The author does an excellent job of breaking down complex financial concepts into manageable steps that any business owner can follow. The emphasis on presenting revenue in a way that highlights stability and long-term value is particularly useful, as it addresses a common concern among buyers: the sustainability of the business after the sale.

Step 2: Operational Excellence is a thorough and practical guide for business owners looking to optimize their operations in preparation for a sale. The author does an excellent job of drawing parallels between maintaining a home's systems and ensuring that a business's operations are running smoothly, making the concept of operational excellence relatable and easy to grasp. One of the strengths of this section is its emphasis on the critical role that systems play in de-risking the business from its owner. By advocating for the implementation of key tools like Customer Relationship Management (CRM) and Project Management (PM) systems, the author underscores how vital it is to have structured processes in place. This section is likely to leave readers feeling more confident and equipped to optimize their operations, ensuring their business is positioned for a successful and lucrative exit.

Step 3: Resource Maximization is a practical and insightful section that addresses the often-overlooked aspects of running a lean and efficient business. One of the section's standout aspects is its frank discussion about workforce efficiency and the "family factor." The author acknowledges the difficulty of letting go of close-knit or long-standing employees, especially family members, while balancing the need to make tough decisions for the greater good of the business. This section offers a well-rounded guide to maximizing business resources, with clear, actionable steps that can significantly improve a company's financial health. The blend of strategic advice, real-world examples, and practical tools make this a valuable read for business owners looking to optimize their operations in preparation for a successful exit.

Step 4: Cognitive Automation section provides a strong case for the transformative power of automation in small and medium-sized businesses. By comparing automation to a smart home, the author effectively makes the concept relatable and emphasizes how technology can drive efficiency, scalability, and profitability. What makes this section stand out is the balance between high-level concepts and actionable steps. The author begins by illustrating automation success stories from giants like Tesla and Amazon, which helps build credibility and aspiration. However, the real value comes from the practical advice for small businesses, such as process mapping, automating basic functions like HR and financial management, and using tools for real-time data dashboards. For instance, the example of a staffing firm that saved hundreds of hours and millions of dollars by automating candidate submissions is a powerful testament to how even basic automation can yield massive returns. By positioning automation as an investment in the future of the business, the author reinforces the idea that embracing AI and RPA can significantly boost both productivity and value, making a strong case for why this should be a priority for any business looking to scale and sell.

Step 5: Expansion Dynamics, serves as a powerful conclusion to the "Exit by FORCE" methodology by highlighting the importance of a strong, visible presence for attracting potential buyers. The focus is on creating a perception of growth potential. It reinforces the idea that the presentation and perception of your business are just as important as its operational and financial health when positioning for a sale. The rec-ommendations around refining your digital presence, building strategic partnerships, and offering a vision for future growth provide practical steps to making your business irresistible to acquirers. The emphasis on controlling how your business is perceived makes this section a key piece of the overall exit strategy

The Final section of this episode, FORCE Unleashed, as a motivational and visionary finale to the FORCE framework. It successfully empha-sizes the transformative power of the methodology, promising sig-nificant rewards for those who follow through. The narrative creates excitement and portrays the success stories of past entrepreneurs who implemented the approach, driving home the value of staying commit-ted to the steps provided. However, the author also wisely tempers the optimism with realism, acknowledging that some may fail to capital-ize on this potential due to common pitfalls. This balanced perspective adds credibility to the promise of the FORCE methodology. This is an inspiring conclusion to the FORCE methodology, blending optimism with practicality. It motivates readers to take control of their business destiny while providing reassurance that those who follow the steps can unlock immense value.

In the final episode of this book, "Your Focus Determines Your Reality", the author emphasizes the critical importance of focus in achieving a successful business exit. By maintaining clarity and determination, busi-ness owners can align their actions with their goals, ensuring that each decision moves them closer to their desired outcome. The episode cat-egorizes small business exits into four types: *Explorers* who are curi-ous but unprepared, *Brokers* who rely on external agents, *Desperate Sellers* who struggle to find buyers, and those who *Exit By FORCE*— well-prepared and in control of the entire process. The author stresses that many business owners fall into traps, often because they are inex-perienced, unprepared, or over-rely on brokers who don't have aligned incentives. By contrast, those who follow the FORCE methodology, meticulously stage their business for sale, and take control of negotia-tions, can command higher values and more favorable terms.

The episode's weaker point, if any, could be its broad discussion on the team-building aspect. While the advice to surround oneself with experts is sound, it could benefit from more concrete examples of what roles and specific expertise are essential for a successful exit. Additionally, while the episode warns against relying on brokers and other external agents who may not have the business owner's best interests at heart, it could offer more detailed advice on how to vet and select trustworthy advisors.

The episode serves as a practical and motivational guide for business owners who are nearing the final stages of selling their business. It underscores the importance of proper preparation, staying focused, and not letting emotions or inexperience get in the way of achieving a successful and lucrative exit. The emphasis on taking control of the process is crucial, as it reminds readers that they can dictate the terms of their exit rather than being passive participants.

Overall, this book is an empowering and insightful guide that leaves readers with a clear understanding of what it takes to exit a business successfully. The author's focus on meticulous preparation, consistent effort, and strategic thinking makes this episode a valuable resource for any business owner looking to maximize the value of their business and exit on their own terms. The episode is both practical and motivational, providing the tools and mindset necessary to make the business exit journey a successful one.

– Harisrikanth Narayanan,
Book Reviewer

ENDNOTES

1. Family Business Institute. "Succession Planning Statistics." Family Business Institute. Accessed July 2024. https://www.familybusinessinstitute.com/succession-planning-statistics/.

2. Skolnik, Jesi, and Adam Hardy. "What Is the Great Wealth Transfer?" Money, April 3, 2023. Accessed July 2024. https://money.com/what-is-the-great-wealth-transfer/.

3. "The Great Wealth Transfer." The Week, April 12, 2023. Accessed July 2024. https://theweek.com/personal-finance/the-great-wealth-transfer.

4. Buffett, Warren. "Warren Buffett Discusses Will in Rare Letter." The Wealth Advisor, 22 Nov. 2023. Accessed July 2024. The Wealth Advisor.

5. Romberg, Stacey. "What We Can Learn From Warren Buffett's Estate Planning." Stacey Romberg, 3 Mar. 2020. Accessed July 2024. Stacey Romberg.

6. BizBuySell. "2021 Insight Report." BizBuySell. Accessed July 2024. https://www.bizbuysell.com/insight-report.

7. "2021 IBBA Market Pulse Survey Report." International Business Brokers Association. Accessed July 2024. https://www.ibba.org/market-pulse.

8. Smyth, Lisa. "Why Do Most Small Business Acquisitions Fail?" Axial, August 20, 2020. Accessed July 2024. https://www.axial.net/forum/why-do-most-small-business-acquisitions-fail/.

9. Phys.org. "Steve Jobs Helped Build Pixar with Vision, Cash." October 7, 2011. Accessed July 2024. https://phys.org/news/2011-10-steve-jobs-pixar-vision-cash.html.

10. Plunkett, Luke. "How Steve Jobs Changed the Course of Animation History." Kotaku, August 24, 2011. Accessed July 2024. https://kotaku.com/how-steve-jobs-changed-the-course-of-animation-history-5833739.

11. Iger, Robert. The Ride of a Lifetime: Lessons Learned from 15 Years as CEO of the Walt Disney Company. New York: Random House, 2019.

12. Tangermann, Victor. "Musk Admits Automation At Tesla Factory Was a Bad Idea." Futurism, April 13, 2018. Accessed July 2024. https://futurism.com/musk-automation-bad-idea.

13. Wells, Anna. "Tesla's Musk Admits to Over-Automating: 'Humans Are Underrated'." Thomasnet, January 27, 2019. Accessed July 2024. https://www.thomasnet.com/insights/tesla-s-musk-admits-to-over-automating-humans-are-underrated.

14. Büchel, Bettina, and Dario Floreano. "Tesla's Problem: Overestimating Automation, Underestimating Humans." IMD. Accessed July 2024. https://www.imd.org/research-knowledge/articles/teslas-problem-overestimating-automation-underestimating-humans/.

15. "Financial Optimization for Small Businesses." Forbes. Published April 5, 2022. Accessed July 2024. https://www.forbes.com/sites/financial-optimization.

16. Gitman, Lawrence J., and Chad J. Zutter. Principles of Managerial Finance. 15th ed., Pearson, 2018.

17. Brigham, Eugene F., and Joel F. Houston. Fundamentals of Financial Management. 15th ed., Cengage Learning, 2019.

18. Morningstar. "When Will the Fed Start Cutting Interest Rates?" April 29, 2024. Accessed July 2024. https://www.morningstar.com/articles/1119077/when-will-the-fed-start-cutting-interest-rates.

19. Trading Economics. "United States Fed Funds Interest Rate." April 10, 2024. Accessed July 2024. https://tradingeconomics.com/united-states/interest-rate.

20. NerdWallet. "Average Business Loan Interest Rates: July 2024." Accessed July 2024. https://www.nerdwallet.com/article/small-business/average-business-loan-interest-rates.

21. Finder.com. "Current Business Loan Interest Rates: SBA, Term Loans (April 2024)." Accessed April 2024. https://www.finder.com/current-business-loan-interest-rates.

22. Apple. "Apple Reports First Quarter Results." April 29, 2024. Accessed July 2024. https://www.apple.com/newsroom/2024/04/apple-reports-first-quarter-results/.

23. Treasure. "A Look Inside Apple Cash Management." May 14, 2021. Accessed July 2024. https://www.treasurefi.com/blog/apple-cash-management.

24. Vanguard. "Vanguard Federal Money Market Fund (VMFXX)." Accessed July 2024. https://investor.vanguard.com/investment-products/mutual-funds/profile/vmfxx.

25. Bogleheads.org. "VMFXX Interest Rate." May 4, 2024. Accessed July 2024. https://www.bogleheads.org.

26. "The Importance of Operational Excellence." Harvard Business Review. Published January 20, 2023. Accessed July 2024. https://hbr.org/2023/01/operational-excellence.

27. Liker, Jeffrey K. The Toyota Way: 14 Management Principles from the World's Greatest Manufacturer. McGraw-Hill, 2004.

28. Womack, James P., Daniel T. Jones, and Daniel Roos. The Machine That Changed the World: The Story of Lean Production. Free Press, 2007.

29. Peppers, Don, and Martha Rogers. Managing Customer Experience and Relationships: A Strategic Framework. 3rd ed., Wiley, 2016.

30. Kumar, V. Customer Relationship Management: Concepts and Technologies. 3rd ed., Springer, 2018.

31. Verzuh, Eric. The Fast Forward MBA in Project Management. 5th ed., Wiley, 2015.

32. Kerzner, Harold. Project Management: A Systems Approach to Planning, Scheduling, and Controlling. 12th ed., Wiley, 2017.

33. "Resource Maximization Techniques." Entrepreneur. Published February 8, 2023. Accessed July 2024. https://www.entrepreneur.com/article/resource-maximization.

34. Hammer, Michael, and James Champy. Reengineering the Corporation: A Manifesto for Business Revolution. HarperBusiness, 2009.

35. Kaplan, Robert S., and David P. Norton. The Balanced Scorecard: Translating Strategy into Action. Harvard Business Review Press, 1996.

36. Isaacson, Walter. Steve Jobs. New York: Simon & Schuster, 2011. Accessed July 2024. https://archive.org/details/stevejobs0000isaa.

37. Voss, Chris, and Tahl Raz. Never Split the Difference: Negotiating As If Your Life Depended On It. New York: Harper Business, 2016.

38. Isaacson, Walter. Elon Musk. New York: Simon & Schuster, 2023.

39. Quinlivan, Joseph. "How Amazon Deploys Collaborative Robots in Its Operations to Benefit Employees and Customers." About Amazon, June 26, 2023. Accessed July 2024. https://www.aboutamazon.com/news/operations/how-amazon-deploys-robots-in-its-operations-facilities.

40. "How Warehouse Automation is Revolutionizing Amazon Logistics." Carbon6. Accessed July 2024. https://www.carbon6.io/blog/warehouse-automation-amazon-logistics.

41. "Introducing Supply Chain by Amazon, an Automated Solution to Help Sellers Quickly and Reliably Ship Products Around the World." About Amazon. Accessed July 2024. https://www.aboutamazon.com/news/operations/introducing-supply-chain-by-amazon.

42. "Cognitive Automation in Business." TechCrunch. Published November 15, 2022. Accessed July 2024. https://techcrunch.com/2022/11/15/cognitive-automation-in-business.

43. Musk, Elon. "The Secret Tesla Motors Master Plan (just between you and me)." Tesla Blog, 2006. Accessed July 2024. https://www.tesla.com/blog/secret-tesla-motors-master-plan-just-between-you-and-me.

44. Bezos, Jeff. "2017 Letter to Shareholders." Amazon, 2017. Accessed July 2024. https://www.amazon.com/p/feature/z6o9g6sysxur57t.

45. "Expansion Dynamics and Business Growth." Inc. Published June 10, 2023. Accessed July 2024. https://www.inc.com/expansion-dynamics.

46. Brynjolfsson, Erik, and Andrew McAfee. The Second Machine Age: Work, Progress, and Prosperity in a Time of Brilliant Technologies. W.W. Norton & Company, 2014.

47. Davenport, Thomas H., and Julia Kirby. Only Humans Need Apply: Winners and Losers in the Age of Smart Machines. Harper Business, 2016.

48. Rowling, J.K. Harry Potter and the Half-Blood Prince. New York: Scholastic, 2005.

www.ingramcontent.com/pod-product-compliance
Lightning Source LLC
Chambersburg PA
CBHW071211210326
41597CB00016B/1770

* 9 7 8 1 9 0 8 7 7 0 7 2 1 *